Contents

Contents

Workbook introduction

1 ILM Super Series study links

This workbook addresses the issues of *Organizational Environment*. Should you wish to extend your study to other Super Series workbooks covering related or different subject areas, you will find a comprehensive list at the back of this book.

2 Links to ILM qualifications

This workbook relates to the following learning outcomes in segments from the ILM Level 3 Introductory Certificate in First Line Management and the Level 3 Certificate in First Line Management.

C3.4   Economic Environment
1   Recognize the importance of economic and political factors for the organization
2   Identify the major economic and political factors which impact upon the organization
3   Appreciate the main economic problems and political measures available to alleviate them

C3.6   European/International Context
1   Appreciate the issues and challenges facing an organization within the global context

2   Identify the membership and institutions of the EU and their impact on the UK and UK business
3   Identify non-EU influences which are significant for UK business
4   Appreciate the effect of exchange rates on the operations of the organization.

3 Links to S/NVQs in Management

This workbook provides you with an understanding of the external environment in which all organizations operate, and helps to develop your competence across a wide range of elements of the Management Standards that are used in S/NVQs in Management. However, it is particularly relevant to developing your competence in:

B1.2   Contribute to the control of resources
D1.1   Gather required information

It is designed to help you develop the following Personal Competences:

- searching for information;
- thinking and taking decisions.

4 Workbook objectives

Sir Alec Douglas Home, British Prime Minister during part of the 1960s, said:

'When I have to read economic documents, I have to have a box of matches and start moving them into position to illustrate and simplify the points to myself'.

If they were honest enough to admit it, many of his successors would have confessed to similar trepidation when faced with mountains of statistical data.

Franklin Roosevelt (President of the USA from 1933 to 1945), charged with leading the USA out of the Great Depression of the 1930s, said 'We have nothing to fear but fear itself. It is fear of the "mysteries" of economics which frequently places far too much power in the hands of politically motivated theorists'.

In reality, practical people the world over understand the basics of economics. A cocoa farmer in West Africa, a British supplier of table lamps to major retailers and the champagne growers of France all understand intuitively the basic economic facts of life. They experience them from day to day and from season to season – just go to any market place anywhere in the country and you will see economic market forces in action.

Economics has an unenviable reputation for being the 'gloomy science', full of concepts unintelligible to anyone other than specialists. In that respect it is no different from the technical specialisms of everybody reading this book. Economists would be just as lost in the jargon jungles of computing, telecommunications, customer relations management, operating theatre practice or risk management unless someone were kind enough to provide them with some guidance.

This book is intended to do just that, and to be an enduring reference work for the basic concepts – the equivalent of Sir Alec's box of matches. As with all complex structures, the economic systems of the UK, the EU and the global economy rest on simple structures which are perfectly intelligible to anyone and everyone.

There is nothing to fear in the study of the economic environment in which your organization works. It is relevant to everything that you do – and is easier to grasp in principle than many complex technical and managerial tasks which you face every day in your normal working life.

4.1 Objectives

When you have completed this workbook you will be better able to:

- list the fundamental factors of production and be able to relate them to your own organization and everyday working life;
- outline the eternal economic problems and the limited range of political measures available to tackle them;
- recognise the important economic and political factors which affect your organization;
- explain the effect of currency exchange rates on organizations in all countries.
- describe the structure of the EU and its impact on the UK and its business;
- identify the influences beyond the EU which are significant for UK business;
- outline the effect which the globalisation of business has on local organizations throughout the world.

5 Activity planner

You may decide to look at the following activities now, so that you can start collecting materials in advance.

- Activity 8 asks you to look at both your own area of responsibility and your organization more generally in terms of the use which it makes of land, capital equipment, labour and raw materials;
- For Activities 9 and 11 you may need to consult your manager, or documents such as annual reports or archive records;
- Activity 13 asks you to look at competition, pricing and subsidies as they affect your own organization;
- Activity 17 asks you to look at the direct and indirect taxes paid by your organization from published accounts or other sources via your manager;
- Activity 22 requires you to look at the way that prices paid by your organization have increased over the past year, or a longer period if practicable;
- Activity 25 asks you to look at the materials and services which your organization imports and exports – you may need assistance from your manager to obtain the information;
- Activity 31 requires information about the MEP who represents the European Parliament seat in which your organization is based.

Some or all of these Activities may provide the basis of evidence for your S/NVQ portfolio. All Portfolio activities and Work-based assignments are sign-posted with this icon.

The icon states the elements to which the Portfolio Activities and Work-based assignment relate.

The Work-based assignment (on pages 99–100) will require that you spend time gathering information and talking to colleagues and people in your workteam. You might like to start thinking about whom you should approach, and perhaps arrange a time to chat with them.

Session A
The economic environment

1 Introduction

The effects of the economic policies of governments and, increasingly, of multinational corporations may seem remote from everyday life. But:

- a government decision to reduce the subsidy paid to a particular industry may show in the closure of facilities such as farms, mines and factories with direct loss of jobs;
- a decision to provide start-up finance may, conversely, lead to the creation of new facilities by overseas companies and the creation of employment in the short or long term;
- the decision of a multinational concern to relocate production facilities from, say, Scotland to China in pursuit – perhaps – of cheaper labour and lower safety, health and welfare standards will have direct local impact on employment and morale in the community.

Whereas it was once common for employees to spend the whole of their working lives with one local employer, generation succeeding generation, this pattern is now very much the exception, even in formerly safe employment in banks, insurance companies, public utilities (electricity, gas, water, telecommunications) and railways.

If you look at the jobs which members of your own family have done since the end of World War Two (1939–1945), the changing pattern will almost certainly become apparent.

Some factors which directly affect people's everyday working lives are beyond the direct control of man. Examples include climate and weather, and natural disasters such as flooding, earthquakes and plagues (whether of locusts or the bubonic plague which killed millions of Europeans in the Middle Ages).

The abolition of individual farms and their forcible grouping into collectives under the communist regime in Russia contributed to famine in the 1930s.

Conversely, in the USA President Roosevelt was tackling the consequences of previous right-wing policies which had little concern for what happened to individuals, and might have led to the rise of socialism in America – the bastion of free enterprise.

In the early twentieth century much of the stock of grapevines in France was wiped out by the phyloxera virus. Wine making, of colossal economic importance and significance to national morale, was affected disastrously. It was eventually rescued by the importation of resistant strains from California – where they had been taken by economic migrants in the previous century.

Economic policies carried to either extreme of the political spectrum can produce profound and often disastrous consequences for organizations and the individuals who work for them.

The UK has never swung to either end of the political spectrum, but the protectionist Corn Laws of the 1830s and 1840s were a contributory factor to famine in Ireland. The result was a mass migration of people to America, and the memory of the famine still influences political attitudes in the twenty-first century, well over 150 years later.

All these issues raise moral, ethical, financial and economic questions to which there are seldom clear cut answers. The following activity illustrates the complexities involved.

Activity 1

8 mins

You have come across a headline in the press that says carpets sold through a major chain of stores in the UK are being produced by child labour (from the age of six upwards) in sweatshops in central Asia. Child workers are preferred to adults because their small hands are claimed to be ideal for tying the tiny knots which give the carpets their undoubted quality. The children are paid a pittance by UK standards. The newspaper reports that there are fears about the long-term effects on the children's eyesight, and there is a risk of their developing arthritis in their fingers.

It would be quite practical for the carpets to be produced by means of power looms in the UK or Belgium. This would provide more employment in those countries, reduce the price to buyers and possibly generate more sales for the retailer. The machine-made carpets would still be of high quality, but would not match the hand-made originals.

However, there would be no chance of alternative employment for the children in Asia and there is no state schooling available to them.

1 Think about this scenario for a while and then suggest at least three reasons which the Asian sweatshop owners might advance for keeping production where it is.

_____

_____

_____

2 In one sentence, give your opinion of what would be the correct course of action. Do not exceed the time allotted to this activity.

_____

_____

_____

_____

The sweatshop owners might argue that:

- there is nothing else for the children to do;
- they are learning a skilled trade;
- their parents are dependent on their income;
- the cost of living is much lower, so they do not need European levels of pay;
- if they can't make carpets they will starve – so there is little point in worrying about their long-term health;
- the quality which their small fingers produce is what the discerning customer wants and is prepared to pay for;
- if sweatshops close, the children together with their immediate families and all the suppliers involved in the trade will suffer hardships unimaginable in a country which has state welfare provision;
- the land around the sweatshops is stony, barren and unsuited to growing crops – but the sheep whose wool is used can make do on the poor pasture which it offers.

You may have thought of other reasons. There will be as many one sentence views of what is the correct solution as there are readers of this workbook. For example, employing the children's parents instead, which would result in only a small increase in costs and actually no reduction in quality. As customers become aware of the conditions in which goods are produced, they may become less willing to buy them.

This case has no solution at a price **willingly affordable** to all parties. Inevitably there will be winners and losers whatever decision the retailer comes to.

The familiar paisley pattern associated with the Scottish town of Paisley and used in shawls, neckties, headscarves and many other goods is in fact an Eastern pattern which the ingenious manufacturers found ways of mass-producing. This created employment in Scotland, but deprived the Eastern craftsmen of at least a part of their market. So there were winners and losers in this real example.

The purpose of this activity was to stress the complexity of economic decision-making and the moral and ethical dimensions which such decisions entail.

2 How economics affects everyone

We will now look at how some of the matters described in the last section may have affected you personally.

Activity 2

2 mins

Think about your own working situation and the influence, for good or ill, that governments, multinationals and natural occurrences have had on it. Describe each influencing factor in the first column, then explain in what way it was an influence for good or ill. You may find that some of the factors have both good and bad influences.

Factor	Influence for good	Influence for ill
Government decision:		
Decision by multinational company:		
Natural occurrence:		

Your experiences will differ widely, but it is very likely that you have been affected by at least one of the influences listed, whatever your job. For example:

■ overseas companies have established factories here as the result of government policy, especially policy involving development grants in areas perceived as economically deprived;

■ some of these companies have gone elsewhere again, as soon as the benefits to them have worn off or new incentives have been offered elsewhere; this has happened in the UK under both Conservative and Labour Governments;

■ policies such as privatization have led to radical changes in employment patterns for millions of people in such industries as mining, transport, public utilities and naval dockyards;

■ anyone involved in food manufacturing will have been affected at some time by bumper harvests or by total crop failures caused by bad weather or disease;

■ policies aimed at improving the health, safety and working conditions of people in Western Europe have had the effect of driving up the costs of employment here compared with developing countries or even with those countries in Eastern Europe which are hoping to join the European Union (EU);

■ changes in taxation policy can influence the ability of people to support charities and reduce the value of the contributions which they make.

These opening sections have invited you to think about the consequences of what is often called macroeconomics – a study of economics that looks at the 'big picture' of world economics. It tries to explain how the human influences of politics, global business decisions, trends in population numbers and consumption interact with influences largely outside the control of man (such as the climate) to build up the picture which the observer can see in total – a bit like a completed jigsaw with all its pieces in place.

It can include situations as diverse as that of young carpet weavers in Central Asia and your own situation. The aim has been to get you to think in terms of the ethical dimension of trade, as well as the objective dimension which can be measured in terms of profit and loss accounts and balance sheet figures.

In general the economic decisions taken by elected governments reflect the attitudes of the voters who have elected them. These are a mixture of:

■ rational decisions arrived at through practical thought processes; and
■ emotional decisions which come from the heart.

The electorate has, over time, the power to influence policy. That is why it is important for all the members of an electorate to take an interest in the economic policies which their government pursues. They will then be in a position to make an informed choice about what general direction is acceptable in policy-making.

It is said that if you ask three economists in a room to recommend a solution to a problem, they will come up with at least four answers. Having begun to see how difficult the choices are, you may decide that this isn't perhaps so surprising.

Joseph de Maistre, a French philosopher who lived from 1753 to 1821 said: 'Each country has the government it deserves'.

3 Factors of production

Factors of production are the three elements which any organization must combine in varying amounts to produce any product or service. No organization, whatever its purpose, can operate without utilizing these three factors. One of the factors is land – for example, the land on which an office factory, hospital or distribution depot is situated.

Activity 3

2 mins

Now from your own experience at work, decide what other two factors are needed in addition to land to produce the goods or services that your own organization provides. The following letters contain the names of all three factors:

LONAATIABLAUDCRPL (17 letters in total)

1 L _ _ _

2 C _ _ _ _ _ _

3 L _ _ _ _ _

You will find the answers on page 118.

You will appreciate that these are very broad categories into which everything used within the world's total economy may be grouped.

The term 'capital' is used to refer to a whole range of physical assets – from a power station to a computer. For convenience such assets are usually expressed in terms of what they would cost to buy or replace. However, money of itself cannot produce goods or services. It has to be used to buy a physical asset – a machine, a vehicle, a piece of computer software, before it can combine with land and labour to produce goods and services.

Activity 4

3 mins

Below is a list of fifteen items used in the production of a good or service. Allocate each of them to one of the three factors of production. You should finish up with five items under each factor.

development site   delivery vehicle   agricultural field   computer

receptionist   economist   combine harvester   shop worker

managing director   garage forecourt   video camera   car park

power station   riverside wharf   itinerant fruit picker

Land	Capital	Labour

You will find an answer to this activity on page 118.

You may have needed to think fairly hard about some of the items where there may be a blurring between capital and land. For example:

- a power station is definitely capital, but the **site** on which it stands is land;
- a garage forecourt is **land** but equipment such as pumps and the overhead canopy are **capital**.

It is perhaps less surprising that all the people listed are labour. But it might be a chastening experience for economists to be listed alongside itinerant fruit pickers. To an economist, both are labour – though one category is no doubt paid much more than the other!

Does all this really matter other than to economists? Well yes it does, both to you and your organization, as you will see from the following activities.

3.1 The pressure to become least cost producer

One of the stated aims of many organizations nowadays is to be the least cost producer in their field, i.e. the producer who produces a product or service at the lowest possible cost in terms of land, capital and labour. This is vital to many commercial companies driven by pressure from supermarket buyers or overseas competition, but it is also true of many other organizations, not only those which are commercial or profit-driven. For example, organizations such as hospitals, schools, local authorities and the courts are required to operate within tight budgets and must look constantly to control their costs.

The way organizations most frequently seek to reduce costs is by:

- replacing one factor of production with a cheaper one, say replacing skilled workers with unskilled ones;
- reducing the cost of an individual factor, such as land – say by moving offices from London to a city where office rents are lower.

There are many ways of reducing costs, as the next activity will demonstrate.

Activity 5 · 5 mins

The Landor company manufactures children's clothes. It sells exclusively to high street retailers who market them under their own brands. Landor is coming under increasing pressure to reduce its prices because its three largest customers are all keen to improve their profit margins.

Landor prides itself on a high quality, machine-made but hand-embroidered product manufactured from soft, durable fabric. The customers insist that the fabric should not be downgraded. All staff are paid the agreed union rates for their work and there is one team leader to every eight staff. The present machinery is running at an average 65% of maximum throughput annually.

Suggest four ways in which Landor could move towards being a least cost producer by changing the costs of its **capital** and **labour** factors of production and the proportions in which they use them.

For practical purposes, there is nothing that they can do about their location in the short term, so the cost of their **land** is fixed.

You may have considered the following options:

Capital

- changing to machine embroidery from hand-sewn embroidery, to reduce the labour cost;
- installing faster machines, or speeding up existing ones, so that fewer operators can process the same output through fewer machines;
- closing approximately 35% of its machines and transferring their production to the remaining 65%. If this were practicable, it would then be running the remaining machines at nearer 100% capacity, resulting in much more efficiency and fewer people;
- finding other work to fill the machines, so that their overheads can be spread over a larger number of items. At present, they have up to 35% spare capacity.

Labour

- switching production to a country where payment rates are lower;
- reducing the level of supervision from 1:8 operators to 1:10 or even 1:12;
- introducing piece work or bonus schemes which offer operators the chance to increase earnings through increased output per worker.

This very simple example shows clearly how important the management of factors of production can be to any organization.

This activity was concerned with capital and labour, so what about the third factor of production, **land**? The UK is one of the most densely populated countries in Europe – less than **half** the size of France, but with a similar population (approaching 60 million in 2002). The mountainous areas of Wales, Scotland, the north of England and Northern Ireland are unsuitable for large towns and are remote from potential markets, increasing the pressure on lower lying areas in all four countries.

It is frequently said that land is the scarcest economic resource because you can't make any more of it. But is this true?

This case illustrates in simple terms what has been happening to so many industries in the UK and elsewhere over the past 50 years. Machinery has become faster and more able to imitate skilled human work. Faster distribution systems world-wide have enabled organizations to look for cheaper labour away from the developed world and to buy good products anywhere on earth.

Activity 6 · 2 mins

Can you think of one or two examples in Europe of countries which have made more land – other than by seizing someone else's!

1 _____

_____

2 _____

_____

Large-scale examples include:

- the polder land of The Netherlands (an even more densely populated country than the UK), where vast tracts of land have been reclaimed from the North Sea and turned into productive farmland;
- the fen country in the English counties of Lincolnshire, Bedfordshire, Norfolk and Cambridgeshire, where similar drainage works changed the romantic – but unproductive – areas of low lying misty marshland into prime agricultural land;
- similar areas of Romney Marsh in Kent and East Sussex which were also once under the sea.

Though these and other examples are very significant, they represent a small proportion of the total land of each country and are very much exceptions to the rule.

The once important, thriving town of Dunwich in Norfolk has disappeared beneath the North Sea, as have whole areas of the Holderness area of East Yorkshire.

Gloomy predictions about climatic change suggest that the North Sea will, in any case, take back equivalent areas in the foreseeable future. Coastal erosion has been wearing away areas around the UK's long coastline for centuries, sometimes flooding whole towns.

So, while the opportunities to make more land are limited, you can put what you have to different uses:

Billy Butlin realized that, following World War One (1914–1918), there were many surplus army camps, some of them sited in potential holiday locations, such as Skegness. On the basis of that observation, he acquired land cheaply and changed its purpose from **military** camp to **holiday** camp. He thus founded the business which still bears his name, has provided holidays for millions of people, and is still the largest employer in Skegness in 2002.

The Gulf State of Dubai is sparsely populated and has abundant land, most of it unusable for most purposes because of the extreme temperatures and desert conditions. However, Dubai is currently a major supplier of oil. It also has an international airport used as a stopover for long-distance flights.

The ruling family decided to turn much of the coastal land into leisure facilities to attract visitors from all over the world. With abundant oil revenues, they could afford to build (and run) air-conditioned hotels, irrigate the desert and create golf courses, race courses and leisure facilities using the sea.

They are looking long-term. The oil will eventually run out, so their intention is to create an alternative economy, based on leisure, sales of duty-free goods, tourism and the international airport.

Both these case studies show how enterprising people can make good alternative use of land, even if they cannot create it.

4 Raw materials

You will have noticed that the three factors of production do not include the raw materials used by organizations.

This is because raw materials are actually consumed and must be replaced continuously if the work is to continue. Take a corned beef plant in Argentina, for instance, tinplate, cattle, corn and seasonings go in one end of the factory and tins of corned beef come out the other end.

If you want more corned beef, you must put in more of each raw material, but the factors of production, i.e. the land on which the buildings stand, the factory equipment and the staff, are all still there ready to process the next batch.

So, while the various factors of production are constant items in the production process, raw materials are consumed and must be provided continuously if the process is to be sustained. The materials vary from one organization to another, but every organization has them.

Activity 7 · 8 mins

Look at the different types of organization listed in the table below, then enter the items from the following list into the appropriate columns. All the items are either factors of production or raw materials.

One answer has been inserted under each organization as an example of what is required.

computerized switchboard	shop assistant	rented garage	football pitch
travelling oven	car park	office space	rented shop
sub editor	X ray machine	print room	customer care assistant
standard letters	goalkeeper	high-speed press	flour and water
goods delivery notes	computer	gymnasium	surgeon
dressings	entrepreneur	practice balls	ink

Organization	Land	Capital	Labour	Raw materials
Hospital	car park			
Call centre				standard letters
Internet marketing firm		computer		
Take-away pizza shop			shop assistant	
Newspaper		high-speed press		
Football club	football pitch			

Studies in the years 2000 and 2001 have shown that the supposed paperless office of the computer age is actually consuming **more** paper – the raw material of commercial life. Vast numbers of emails, management information, advertising materials, etc. are sent electronically, but subsequently printed out.

The answers can be found on page 118. There may be one or two items which you have assigned differently, but most will square with the model provided.

The last activity asked you to think about some of the important factors of production, showing that even the highest paid surgeon or soccer superstar is 'labour' in economic terms.

The next activity brings together many of the points that have been covered under factors of production and raw materials.

Activity 8

S/NVQ B1.2

Portfolio of evidence

This Activity may provide the basis of appropriate evidence for your S/NVQ portfolio. If you are intending to take this course of action, it might be better to write your answers on separate sheets of paper.

Think about the activities of your own organization and list the principal factors of production and raw materials used:

■ in your own area of responsibility;
■ for your total site or the organization generally.

For many organizations, this could produce a very long list, so please use your discretion to prioritize them and list only the top five or so in each category.

	Land	Capital	Labour	Raw materials
Your area of responsibility				
Your site or organization generally				

4.2 Renewable and non-renewable resources

Renewable resources

Renewable resources are raw materials which can reproduce themselves, given suitable conditions – such as food or fuel crops, trees, animals and fish. Power from wind, tides and the flow of rivers are also renewable, as is solar power captured directly from the sun.

However, as a result of the way the world has been 'managed' for many years now, even renewable resources are under threat or have already been reduced to dangerously low levels. For example:

Economics is frequently called the gloomy science, at least in part because it forces people to face issues that they hope will go away if ignored. But the issues won't, even if the resources do.

- the North American buffalo was all but made extinct by unfettered hunting in the nineteenth century;
- stocks of fish in the oceans are under serious threat.
- timber has been plundered to such an extent from the rain forests of South America and South East Asia that another seemingly limitless resource could be threatened;
- the desertification of areas in several continents which could once grow food crops, another renewable resource is proceeding at an alarming rate.

In the case study about Dubai, reference was made to the oil – on which the state's wealth rests – eventually running out. Many or the world's resources are in this category. That simple fact has a profound influence on economic policies and the way in which all organizations must manage their affairs.

Non-renewable resources

Non-renewable resources are in an even more dire situation. These are resources that do not reproduce themselves, such as coal, oil and natural gas – the very sources of power which literally drove the industrial revolution which began in the eighteenth century.

Many of these resources are running down or having to be extracted from increasingly remote and expensive sites.

No wonder that economics is often called the 'gloomy science'! However, there is no way of avoiding the consequences of these macroeconomic factors; they affect everyone sooner or later, if only because the prices of all the items concerned – or products containing them – will be driven relentlessly upwards.

For example, dwindling fish stocks have led to steep price increases for fish and chips. As cod, plaice and haddock become scarcer, their price increases to reflect their scarcity and the increased costs of landing them from more remote fisheries.

5 The price mechanism

Henry Ford said that the ideal product:

'costs a dime (10 cents) sells for a dollar **and** every home must have one'.

He was right when he said it – and just as right 100 years or more later.

Each of the factors of production has a price, as do the raw materials which each organization uses.

- In simple terms, the more abundant the factor or material, the less it will cost.
- The scarcer it becomes, the more expensive it becomes.
- If there is no market for it, i.e. if no one wants it, then scarcity will have little or no effect on price. For example, if fur-bearing animals are scarce, but people give up wearing fur for ethical reasons, then the price of fur will not be high.

Let's look at the price mechanism in relation to each factor of production.

5.1 Land

The price of land varies according to its scarcity.

Skyscrapers were built in American cities because it seemed that every business must be in Manhattan or a particular, limited area of Chicago – so the only way was up.

If you've ever flown over the UK at night, the contrast between brilliantly lit conurbations like London, Birmingham, Manchester and Glasgow and the darkness of rural counties like Shropshire, Cumbria and Lincolnshire is vividly apparent.

Much earlier, many British and European towns acquired the typically narrow shop fronts onto the high street which they still exhibit today. It was essential to display your wares in a particular area of the town, so property values increased and it was cheaper to have long, narrow shops than wide, shallow ones. Local tax policies also encouraged this approach.

Agricultural land varies in price according to what you can do with it. Prime arable land, found in the eastern counties of England, will grow high-value crops like bread-making wheat. It costs substantially more than hill pasture in Wales which is suitable only for cattle or sheep farming and produces lower returns per acre.

In times of agricultural depression, the price of farmland of all types will tend to fall. Sometimes farmers will build up their holdings in anticipation of a later recovery, just as dealers will buy stocks and shares when they believe them to have bottomed out.

The UK has particularly expensive land in world terms because of its high population density and the concentration of people and business activity in a few areas.

The price of housing, office space and industrial land in the conurbations simply reflects competition between buyers of land who must live or operate in those areas.

Other places where land prices are always high and rising include Hong Kong, Singapore and Monaco. All are small places, with little or no chance of expanding.

Activity 9

10 mins

S/NVQ B1.2, D1.1

This Activity may provide the basis of appropriate evidence for your S/NVQ portfolio. If you are intending to take this course of action, it might be better to write your answers on separate sheets of paper.

Think about your own organization and any effect which land prices have had on its present location. For example, has it always been where it is now, or has it relocated from a city centre site to an industrial estate, or to offices in a satellite town?

Has it sold a prime site in a city centre for development and used the cash generated to fund the move to cheaper premises in terms of rent and rates?

There are any number of possibilities, but so many organizations have relocated because of increasing land prices, that yours may well have been affected. List any land/price related issues which you can identify.

_____

_____

_____

_____

5.2 Capital

As you have seen, the definition of capital takes in massive items such as agricultural machinery, power stations and operating theatres through to small items such as computers and other office equipment.

The price of some equipment, particularly in data processing, has moved downwards over many years, and this is partly why so many office-based jobs are now dependant upon it – or have been replaced by it.

The price of many items of machinery has increased because of the safety features which are legally required by governments.

The cost of buses is increased by the requirement to provide access for the disabled, a factor which may produce increased income through disabled people being able to use the vehicles.

The price of some capital items increases because they are built from materials which are themselves scarce or expensive to manufacture, such as aluminium and titanium used in aircraft construction.

5.3 Labour

Wages, salaries, piece-work rates, commissions, royalties and fees are all ways of expressing the price of labour. You may be able to think of others.

The price of labour is affected by its scarcity or abundance in the same way as the price of the other factors of production.

The wages of agricultural labourers increased substantially in the Middle Ages after the Black Death wiped out a large percentage of all such workers in a few terrible years.

If you think back to the children in Activity 1, they are in plentiful supply and so can demand only minimal wages. Even though their work is skilled, the skills they possess can be readily taught to other children. In the absence of any regulation of child labour, there is no reason in **economic** terms why they should be paid any more in an economy where wages are generally low and unemployment typically high.

In the UK, the indigenous population is stable and there are strict rules about what work children can undertake. There is also strict minimum wage legislation which an employer cannot breach, even if employees are prepared to work for less. Unlike in poorer countries, there are also 'on costs' which increase the price of labour. These are the costs that are over and above the direct costs of wages or salary, and it is worth identifying them.

Activity 10 · 2 mins

List the typical on costs which an employer must bear in addition to the direct price which an employee charges for his or her labour.

_____

_____

_____

_____

_____

The answer can be found on page 118.

The price of labour is more sensitive a subject than that of capital or land because even the highest paid individuals tend to believe that they are worth **at least** what they receive now – if not more. How often have you heard a footballer, a show business personality, the chairman of a public company or a politician propose taking a pay cut, however highly they are paid? Have **you** ever believed you were overpaid for what you were doing and asked the organization you worked for to give you a pay cut?

Rationally, if the price of labour increases beyond what an employer is prepared to pay, then that employer will try either to:

- find someone else prepared to work for less, possibly in another country, as increasing numbers of employers are doing; or
- replace labour with capital – bigger, faster machinery, or automatic systems which can duplicate at least some of the tasks which human beings typically undertake.

Human resources have a maximum affordable price, just like any other factor of production. It is a hard fact of economic life.

One American multinational company has put forward the idea of a 'floating factory' which can sail from port to port in pursuit of the optimum combination of an able workforce willing to work for the lowest wages. This graphic concept, though it may never become reality, shows just how companies think in the twenty-first century.

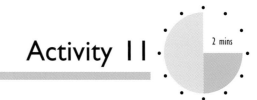

Activity 11

2 mins

Portfolio of evidence

S/NVQ B1.2, D1.1

Look once again at your own area of responsibility and your organization more widely. List examples where the organization has substituted capital for labour, moved activities abroad, reduced manning levels or substituted lower-paid workers to do routine jobs. It has happened so frequently in recent years that you are very likely to find examples equivalent to:

■ converting shops or garage forecourts into self service;
■ establishing hotels with no human receptionists;
■ assigning work formerly done by nurses to ward orderlies;
■ introducing automated telephone answering systems to deal with routine transactions;
■ introducing driver-only buses.

_____

_____

_____

_____

_____

5.4 The price mechanism and competition

Mixed or 'market' economy

In a typical **mixed** economy the government retains responsibility for matters such as security, education, social services, law enforcement and health services, while the majority of goods and services are provided by private organizations which need to make a reasonable level of profit to survive.

The combined prices of all the factors of production and the costs of raw materials all feed through into the price which producers charge to the eventual users of their products.

In 'mixed' or 'free market' economies, such as those in the UK and Western Europe, the consumer has a choice as to:

■ who to buy a product or service from;
■ whether to buy it at all.

For example, if you are thinking about using a mobile phone, you can choose from a wide range of companies, all of whom claim to be the best. **You** can decide which is the best for you, or you can choose not to have a mobile phone at all.

If you believe electricity is too expensive, or you don't like your present supplier, you can change supplier or move to natural or bottled gas, oil, coal, wood fires – according to your needs and desires. You are not stuck with a particular supplier who can tell you to take it or leave it if you complain. You don't even need a good reason to change, you can do so on a whim.

Activity 12 ·   2 mins

Can you think of one commodity in the UK which:

- is essential to life, i.e. we should die rapidly if deprived of it;
- is available from only one supplier in any given area of the country;
- is provided by a private, profit-making organization.

_____

_____

_____

_____

_____

The answer can be found on page 119. You may have thought of a different example. The answer given touches on the subject of monopoly, which will be expanded on shortly.

There are any number of choices available in a mixed economy for the basic human needs of food, shelter and clothing. For example:

- if you own some land, you can grow at least some of your food for yourself – and keep some chickens as well;
- you can buy or rent a house, or find a room in someone else's house if you prefer. If you do decide to buy, then there are many mortgage options available;
- for clothing, again, there are countless shops, mail order and Internet businesses from whom you can buy. Or you can buy materials such as wool, cotton and silk and make at least some of them for yourself.

It is competition between organizations which prevents them from charging what they please and maximizing their profits at your expense.

Command economy
Under a state-directed or 'command' economy, such as those of the USSR and the People's Republic of China under communism, the State acquired the means of:

- production;
- distribution;
- exchange (in effect, banking).

The state exercised a monopoly over every aspect of people's lives for many years. In the latter part of the twentieth century, both these huge countries have moved towards a mixed economy.

5.5 Monopoly

But what would happen if there should be only **one** supplier, or if a number of large suppliers get together and agree to charge the same price? From their point of view, that makes everything much simpler:

- they can plan ahead on the basis of known prices and a guaranteed market share;
- they need have no fear of being undercut by a rival;
- they can fix the price to produce whatever return they like on the factors of production which they use, and maximize their profit if they so desire;
- they really can tell people to take it or leave it if they complain about their goods, services or prices.

Monopoly prevents the price mechanism from working. It is outlawed or severely constrained in the UK, as described in the answer to Activity 12.

The former state monopolies which were privatized in the late twentieth century are all regulated by independent bodies. For example, in the USA, there has also been legislation to eliminate or minimize the effects of private monopolies through the anti-trust laws. These attempt to prevent large private businesses getting together and rigging the market.

Though monopoly seems a most attractive condition if you are a supplier, it is harder to sustain than many hopeful monopolists have thought. This piece of economists' wisdom explains one of the basic flaws with all monopolies:

> 'the fortunate monopolist can charge what price he chooses,
> but if he cannot sell enough, he doesn't gain, he loses'.

The sad facts of life from the monopolist's point of view are that:

- competition will always be attracted to move in on a monopoly, tempted by the artificially high profit margins it has generated;
- there are very few products for which consumers cannot find a substitute;
- consumers resent monopolistic practices and, unless they are enforced by law (as under communist regimes), will try hard to find ways of undermining them.

A manufacturer had patented a process for making speciality papers. It was the only UK manufacturer for a product which many offices had to have. It charged accordingly and for some years made profits which far exceeded what its costs of production would justify.

Overseas manufacturers could not breach the patent but, seeing a profitable market, developed alternative products. Though technically not as good, they did the job adequately at a substantially lower price and still yielded an acceptable return on their substantial investment. Resentful customers moved in significant numbers to the alternative suppliers and their substantially cheaper new materials.

The monopolist's sales fell and it was forced eventually to cut prices. By that time the highly specialist equipment it had installed was growing old and needed replacement at a cost that was hard to justify in the changed market conditions.

Monopoly, like so many features of economic life which seem permanent, is actually more often a temporary feature. Ultimately, the price mechanism which adjusts demand to supply will have its way, unless the monopoly is sustained by laws or by physical force.

5.6 Subsidy

Subsidies are another mechanism which can distort the price mechanism. Governments through the ages have used them for a wide range of purposes. For example, the European Union (EU) has subsidized agricultural products throughout its existence.

Very often, subsidies have been used for benevolent purposes, for example, to ensure that the poorer people in a country can afford the basic necessities of life, say by:

■ subsidizing the price of bread or other staple foodstuffs;
■ providing low cost housing;
■ providing cheaper heating to people vulnerable to cold, typically older people in a cold climate.

Under subsidized pricing:

■ the consumer does not pay the full market price for the product or service;
■ the producer receives the difference between the subsidized price and the market price from a third party, typically the government.

As an illustration of subsidy at work, imagine that the market price of bread equates to 75 pence per standard 800 gram loaf, but the government decides that the maximum which a defined group of people can afford is 55 pence per loaf. Then the government will pay the balance of 20 pence per loaf to the producer out of its general taxation revenues.

You might think this is a proper use of subsidy, provided that the wealthier members of society agree to provide the funds which the government requires to pay the difference. But it distorts the normal price mechanism – and subsidies can be used for less ethical purposes, particularly to protect local industries (such as farming and steel production) from overseas competition, perhaps from developing countries where the costs of the factors of production are lower.

The USA, the avowed home of free enterprise and the market economy, actually provides heavy subsidies to its farmers to make them competitive with imported food. Because the US economy is so huge, this has the effect of distorting the whole world economy.

In 2002 the collapse of a number of media companies in the UK and Europe threatened the future of some of the most famous football clubs in countries such as Germany, Spain, Italy and the UK.

For years, teams have depended on TV income for a major part of their income. Much of that income has been used to pay wages to players, sometimes of millions of pounds (or euros) per annum. Meanwhile, the number of spectators able and willing to attend matches has fallen and matches have been scheduled to suit the TV companies rather than the fans.

By 2002 TV advertising revenues were falling, pay-to-view channels had found that the majority of potential viewers would **not** pay to watch most matches – and so the incomes of the broadcasters fell dramatically.

TV revenues had in effect subsidised businesses, most of which were not operating in anything like a commercial fashion. A large percentage of that subsidy went in labour cost – players' wages – and straight out of the game. The huge revenues from the years of plenty largely disappeared, and insufficient reserves (of money, not players) were created for the lean years which might follow when the TV companies offer smaller deals to reflect their smaller revenues.

Had the clubs operated under normal price mechanisms over the good years, their finances would almost certainly be in more reasonable shape. Their wages bills would certainly be more affordable.

This example of a subsidy provided by commercial organizations shows how much it can distort things and encourage the recipients to live in a fool's paradise. There could be no philanthropic purpose for subsidizing the life styles of football players. So, as soon as the expected revenues for the TV companies did not materialize, their own future was threatened and they pulled the plug.

In Germany, there was a suggestion that the federal government should effectively subsidize the clubs affected. Given that four million German people were unemployed in 2002, the idea did not prove universally popular. Most of them would earn less in a lifetime than many football players are paid in one year – and many Germans have no interest in football.

This look at subsidies began by discussing their use to help poorer people. It widened into their use to protect activities like farming or steel production which a country believes is vital to protect for strategic or political reasons. However desirable that may be, the use of subsidies always distorts the working of the price mechanism which is at the heart of capitalism and mixed economies such as that of the UK.

The football case study shows that subsidies also appear in surprising places. Wherever they crop up, they distort the working of the price mechanism – which in the long term will create problems of one kind or another.

The next activity will ask you to look at the factors of price, competition and subsidy as they affect your own organization.

Activity 13

S/NVQ B1.2, D1.1

This Activity may provide the basis of appropriate evidence for your S/NVQ portfolio. If you are intending to take this course of action, it might be better to write your answers on separate sheets of paper.

Please identify for your own organization:

■ who your chief direct competitors are. If you work for an organization such as the National Health Service, you can still be in competition with private sector or overseas providers – there are surprisingly few organizations which have no competition at all.

■ how you believe that your prices compare with those of your direct competitors. This may be more or less easy to discover, according to what your organization does, and it may be necessary for you simply to state your impression of the position.

■ any indirect competition you know of. For example, can people change from your product to another, in the same way as they can swap from electricity to gas, from tube trains to buses or from reading papers to listening to radio news?

■ any subsidies involved which affect your organization. Many organizations will not have any, but the football case study shows that subsidies can turn up in unexpected places.

_____

_____

_____

_____

_____

So far in this session we have looked at:

■ the factors of production;
■ their prices;
■ the price mechanism, which normally keeps supply and demand in balance;
■ issues of subsidized pricing and monopolies – public or private – which distort it.

These economic concepts are fundamental to understanding all economic issues within your own organization and beyond it. Keeping them in mind will help you understand all the larger issues which will be looked at in the remainder of this Session and in Session B.

6 The economic levers which governments use

Governments throughout the world try to control the remorseless interplay of supply and demand with varying degrees of success.

Modern governments seem obsessed with economics, but in reality they have far less power than they would like to have.

■ They cannot influence natural phenomena which lead to good or bad harvests or make mines and oil fields unworkable.
■ They frequently do not understand the methods and the technology employed by multinational companies in pursuing their own independent aims.
■ They are in office typically for four or five years and always have an eye to the next election. Many of the economic trends they are endeavouring to influence have much longer cycles.

■ Modern developed world economies are so complex, so inter-related, so dependent on energy and so prone to change that it is impossible for anyone to predict what will happen with any degree of accuracy.

Fiscal and monetary policies are often referred to as 'economic levers' which the Government can use to move the UK's enormous economy in the direction it wants it to go. Changes in taxation policy or interest rates bear on the economy in the same way as a physical lever is used to move a heavy weight. The longer the lever, the greater its potential effect on the weight being moved. So, the greater the movement in tax or interest rates up or down, the greater the potential effect on people's spending and saving decisions.

6.1 Fiscal policy

The term 'fiscal policy' refers to the taxes which governments impose to raise money for spending on defence, health, education, social services and other provisions (such as EU member governments' contribution to centralized EU expenditure).

There are basically two types of taxation:

■ direct (progressive) taxation;
■ indirect (regressive) taxation.

Direct taxation

This is taxation which increases as the income or wealth of individuals or organizations increases. It is frequently called **progressive taxation** – the more you earn, the more you pay.

Activity 14

2 mins

Name two or three direct taxes which are raised by the UK government.

_____

_____

_____

_____

You almost certainly named income tax for individuals and corporation tax for companies, which rise as income rises. In the case of individuals, different rates of tax are applied to different bands of income and so take some account of individuals' ability to pay.

If you have no income, you pay nothing; if your income is relatively high, you pay tax at a higher rate in the pound on the higher part of your taxable income.

National Insurance Contributions (NICs), paid by individuals and employers, are also a form of direct taxation. They again rise as income rises, but in their case only until a fixed upper limit is reached. Stamp duty (paid on property and other capital transactions) and inheritance tax are also forms of direct, progressive taxation.

By increasing or reducing rates of direct taxation, governments can control how much of their earnings individuals and organizations actually keep. This will affect countless decisions on expenditure, which in turn affects the level of economic activity.

Indirect taxation

Indirect taxation takes no account of people's ability to pay and is related to the value of the goods or services which they consume. It is often called 'regressive' tax, because it bears most heavily on individuals with the lowest incomes.

For example, the council tax which people pay to their local authority for a dwelling is based on an estimate of the value of that dwelling. There is a banding system into which all properties, from a croft to a castle, are fitted.

- It makes no difference whether you earn nothing, £15,000 a year or £150,000 a year – you will still pay the same council tax for a Band C property in a given area.
- Poorer people may be given relief in one way or another, but that does not affect the basic nature of the tax, and is another example of subsidy for public policy purposes.

Activity 15

2 mins

List two or three other examples of indirect taxation.

_____

_____

_____

You most probably listed such items as Value Added Tax (VAT), excise duties payable on alcohol and tobacco, and the special petroleum tax added to car fuel. There are many others to choose from, including vehicle road fund licences, business rates and effectively the licence fee payable to the BBC. What they all have in common is that they take no account of ability to pay.

6.2 Every government's dilemma

Two surveys of public opinion were conducted within two weeks of each other. In the first, respondents were asked: 'Would you pay more for a better health service?'. Seventy percent said 'yes'. In the second, the question was 'Do you want taxes to come down?'. To this, 80% responded 'yes'.

It is every government's dilemma that the electorate wants more expenditure on public services, but resents paying taxes. A majority seem to wish to have their cake and eat it and demand that governments keep on baking the cakes, even though they won't provide them with money to buy the flour, sugar, eggs and fat.

In recent times, electors seem especially to resent direct taxes which show up every week or month on their pay slips as Pay As You Earn (PAYE) deductions. This is probably why governments of all political colours have tended to shift the burden from direct to indirect taxation. After all, you don't have to buy alcohol, or petrol, or eat in restaurants, do you? So you can choose whether or not to pay the tax.

Well of course, it isn't that simple and, for many people, there is no choice but to consume at least some of the items caught by such indirect taxes as VAT. We all have to live somewhere, travel to work, buy clothes, heat our homes – all of which attract indirect taxation in one form or another.

Would governments do better to be more honest with the electorate by explaining that, while demand for health care and education can increase for ever, they can only spend ultimately what voters are prepared to let them take by way of taxation? Everyone reading this workbook is likely to be an elector, so you can judge for yourselves how you would react.

Edmund Burke, the eighteenth century reformer and philosopher said simply:

'In all forms of government the people is the true legislator'.

There seems to be no solution to the dilemma of governments as long as they face the hurdle of re-election every four or five years as in the UK. Honesty has not proved to be the best policy in the past. On the other hand, promising what you cannot deliver builds up resentment and accusations of stealth taxes when you shift from progressive direct taxes towards regressive indirect ones.

Governments can shift the tax burden towards the corporation tax (which is paid by organizations who do not have voting power in the way that individuals do). But corporations can vote with their feet by taking their businesses overseas or ceasing to invest here, thus threatening employment prospects – which will again rebound on the government.

If you remember the American company's vision of the floating factory, you'll see that the threat is real. Electorates do not like high unemployment any more than they like high taxes, and it is costly to governments.

6.3 Monetary policy

Monetary policy is the means through which governments control the economy by regulating interest rates. Money, like everything else, has its price. This is expressed as the percentage interest rate which you must pay to any lender who advances you money.

Within days of taking office in 1997, the Labour Government gave authority to the Bank of England to determine the base rate through its independent Monetary Policy Committee (MPC) which meets at the beginning of each month. This decision was welcomed by most commentators and it seems likely that future governments of any party will retain the system. Its perceived advantage is that it reduces the amount of political influence over a crucial economic decision.

In the UK, all interest rates charged by commercial borrowers are by custom linked to the Bank of England base rate, nowadays reviewed each month. The MPC's task is to review inflationary trends against set criteria. It then sets a base rate aimed at keeping the measured rate of inflation within the tolerance limits set.

The Government also borrows money to finance part of its expenditure, and is affected by the interest rates which it must pay to lenders. Each year, it estimates what it needs to borrow, a figure which is called the Public Sector Borrowing Requirement (PSBR).

Like any other borrower, the more the government borrows, the more interest it must pay, and the smaller the amount it has available to spend on other areas. Rising interest rates on the huge sums borrowed can have a significant effect on government finances and can hit spending on desirable projects in education, training, health, public transport, and so on.

Effects of interest rates on exchange rates

Rising interest rates will also tend to increase the value of sterling against currencies such as the dollar and the euro. This makes our exports relatively expensive and can encourage people to import foreign goods or take more overseas holidays.

Reducing interest rates has the opposite effect. This may help UK exporters but make imports and the cost of overseas travel more expensive.

6.4 How does all this affect me and the organization I work for?

The combined effects of fiscal (i.e. taxation) policies and monetary policies directly or indirectly affect every individual and every organization.

Let's begin by looking at the personal impact of the government's use of its economic levers.

Activity 16   5 mins

Write down two possible consequences for yourself of:

1   increasing direct taxes

_____

_____

2   increasing indirect taxes

_____

_____

3   increasing interest rates

_____

_____

What you wrote will of course reflect your own circumstances and you may wish to keep some aspects of what you have written to yourself.

Here are a few general examples of the effects which you may have covered.

1   Increasing direct taxes
    Increasing direct taxes (such as PAYE and NI) reduces the amount of money available to individuals (i.e. it reduces their disposable income). This can reduce spending, demand for goods and services and possibly lead to increased unemployment. (By contrast, reducing direct taxes may have the opposite effect, but also lead to inflation – which will be discussed in Session B – if too much money is chasing too few goods and services.)

2   Increasing indirect taxes
    Increasing indirect taxes (such as VAT and council tax) takes away money which people otherwise might spend on goods and services. By contrast, reducing indirect taxes may create a substantial amount of disposable income – which might fuel inflation. Such indirect taxes are regressive, they bear more heavily on people with low incomes – which may have undesirable consequences. This can cause governments to spend some of the increased tax revenues on subsidies.

3   Increasing interest rates
    Increasing interest rates may cause you and millions of others to reduce what you spend on goods and services and items paid for by credit card. If you have a mortgage, the interest payable on it will take priority over holidays, new furniture and so on – especially if they too were to be financed on credit. Perhaps you might put more money into high-interest savings accounts. High interest rates may boost the value of sterling. Increased value for the pound sterling might encourage you to take holidays overseas, rather than in Great Britain.

4   Reducing interest rates
    Reducing interest rates might encourage you to buy a more expensive house, or a new car – and to withdraw money from accounts paying poor rates of interest. Low interest rates may result in poor exchange rates against other currencies. A poor exchange rate against the euro may persuade you not to have a holiday abroad.

The impact of fiscal and monetary policy on your organization depends on its legal status. If you work for a public limited company, a plc, there will be published accounts which you can access, or perhaps an employees' report. Many other organizations, including charities, publish annual accounts.

Activity 17

S/NVQ B1.2, D1.1

For your own organization, try to obtain financial details for the last three years from its annual report, other published information or through your manager. Then answer the following questions.

1 How much direct taxation was paid to the Inland Revenue in each year, as:

corporation tax

_____

Employers National Insurance Contributions

_____

2 How much VAT was paid over to Customs and Excise in each year?

_____

3 Is there any mention of the effect of exchange rates on sales and profits?

_____

6.4 Legal measures which affect economic activity

Virtually every law – if not **every** law, has some effect on economic activity. For example, the Health and Safety at Work etc. Act imposes conditions which affect the price of equipment and the costs of employing people, though the Act is not specifically about money.

The entire range of employment law imposes, for social and public policy reasons, conditions of employment which increase costs by comparison with developing countries which often compete with this country in the global labour market.

There are many laws devoted directly to the regulation of economic and financial activity and which do not have direct or indirect financial implications on organizations. Many of them are necessary to protect people from the activities of unscrupulous or reckless company promoters or managers. There have existed throughout history people ready and willing to part other people from their money with the promise of quick profits and low risks – an impossible combination.

The German unemployment figure of over 4 million in January 2003 is believed to be at least in part due to the cost of labour there and the difficulty of dismissing employees, even when their jobs have become redundant. A similar situation exists in France, making many employers reluctant to invest in either country.

A politician said of a proposed investment scheme that:

'it held out a dangerous lure for decoying the unwary to their ruin by a false prospect of gain. The great principle of the project was to raise artificially the value of the stock, by exciting and keeping up a general infatuation and by promising dividends out of funds which would not be adequate to the purpose'.

Against his advice, the politicians voted through the legislation required to launch the scheme and their colleagues in the upper house endorsed it. In three months, the value of the stock soared from £128 per share to £300 and a few months later to £500. At its peak, about a year later, it reached £1050. Then people ceased to believe in the project. The share price tumbled and in a few months had sunk to much less than £2 – about one thousandth of the value at its peak. Thousands of people lost their savings, many committed suicide and there was a threat of civil unrest.

Activity 18

8 mins

Of which scheme do you think the politician was speaking:

- something proposed prior to the Wall Street Crash in the USA in 1929;
- the South Sea Bubble of 1720;
- the prospectus of a new technology company in 1999.

Underline your choice.

At about the time of the Bubble, one company promoter issued a prospectus for the carrying on of a great undertaking 'of Great Advantage', but no-one was to know what it was. It proved of great advantage to **him**, at any rate. He set up a shop in London and took £2,000 – equivalent probably to nearer £2 million in 2002 – after which he promptly vanished.

You will find the answer on page 119.

The politician's remarks could equally well apply to many aspects of the two other speculative booms. Both of them included businesses which had no substance to them and were incapable of making real profits. Their success solely depended on people continuing to pay more and more for their shares, despite their lack of real assets, non-existent profits and, during the Internet boom, frequently minimal sales.

Shares in some Internet companies actually rose faster in value than those in the South Sea Company – suggesting that investors had learned nothing in 250 years. Both led to financial ruin for vast numbers of people and again to many suicides after the Wall Street Crash in 1929, which heralded the Great Depression of the 1930s in the USA.

While most people resent government interference in their lives and many believe that there is generally too much of it, it is essential sometimes to protect people from their own gullibility and greed and to provide punishment for those willing to exploit them.

EXTENSION 1
This extension contains a summary of some of the ways in which the government intervenes in the affairs of organizations.

Ever since 1720 there has been a succession of Companies Acts outlawing or circumscribing monopoly activities and prohibiting unfair trading practices. They are designed to force businesses to operate in a fair and honest way. It has not worked perfectly, because the villains are often cleverer than the legislators. But it is fundamentally important to the prosperity of the entire nation.

Activity 19

3 mins

Why do you think it is so important for business to be carried on within a strong legal framework? What can be the adverse effects if it is not?

_____

_____

_____

_____

_____

_____

You probably answered that if there were no rules, and businesses did exactly as they pleased, then the unscrupulous would exploit every opportunity they could find to separate gullible people from their money. Though the majority of honest business people would not do so, they would become tainted with suspicion. Ultimately, confidence in business would collapse (as happened in 1721 and 1929) and business activity would threaten to grind to a halt, to no one's benefit.

It is impossible to over-estimate the importance of confidence in currencies, in governments and in the competence and honesty of business leaders.

Though businessmen grumble about all the red tape which they are tied up in, the majority of honest ones will accept that much of it is necessary and well intentioned, and scarcely impinges for most of the time on those who conduct their affairs honestly.

7 Key economic issues affecting all organizations

So far, this session has explored many of the basic elements which form the economic climate in which your organization functions. It should help you understand the issues which frequently make the headlines in the financial sections of the press. We now move on to look at some of the major economic issues that face all organizations operating in a mixed market economy.

7.1 The price mechanism

In a free market or mixed economy it is the **price mechanism** which keeps the demand and supply of the three factors of production in balance. The concept is simple:

- if supply outstrips demand, then prices will fall;
- if demand outstrips supply, then prices will rise.

The five topics introduced so far in this session are all examples of the price mechanism at work.

Activity 20 · 3 mins

A market trader had a large stock of bananas on his stall. He had bought them at a good price, because they were nearing the end of their saleable lives. By lunchtime, when he had sold about two thirds of them, it began to rain heavily and the customers disappeared. At three o'clock, the sun reappeared and with it the potential customers, but with only two hours maximum of trading left.

What would you have done if you were the market trader?

_____

_____

A beach ice cream vendor suffered a miserable morning of rain and chilly winds. By two o'clock most of his competitors had abandoned hope for the day and gone home. The weather relented and a glorious hot afternoon brought large numbers to the beach. The nearest cafes were more than ten minutes' hot walk away.

What might the vendor do under these circumstances?

_____

_____

No doubt you suggested that the banana seller should slash his prices and turn as much of his stock into cash as he could, selling it for whatever he could get. A rotting pile of bananas the next morning would be no use to anyone.

The beach vendor, if hard headed enough, might well exploit his local monopoly and raise prices to make back some of his lost profit from the miserable morning, and reward himself for his persistence.

These are two simple examples of market forces and the price mechanism in operation. You've almost certainly experienced similar examples – where you've obtained bargains, or gone away feeling that you've paid through the nose.

Keep these simple examples in mind as you look at the so called 'bigger issues'; at root, all markets behave similarly, if they are not distorted by factors such as subsidy or protectionism.

7.2 Exchange rates

When you travel from one country to another, the rate of exchange which you are offered reflects the purchasing power of each currency. At one time five shillings – now 25p – was often called a 'dollar', dating back to the time when the pound sterling was worth four dollars and would buy four times as much as the dollar would. Since then, the dollar has increased in value until, at the time of writing, the pound is worth around $1 50c, representing a devaluation of around 63% from that £1 = $4 rate.

When you exchange one currency for another, say pounds for euros, you are buying a commodity, just as though you were buying bananas from the market trader. What they cost reflects:

- how badly you want to buy them;
- how keen the seller is to sell them.

This in turn represents their purchasing power when you come to exchange them for goods and services.

This matters enormously to countries such as the UK which import and export goods and services. If the value of the pound falls against the dollar, reflecting weak economic performance here, then we have to export more goods to buy the same amount of goods priced in stronger currencies.

If the pound rises against the dollar, then we need to sell less but our exports become relatively more expensive.

If you have ever visited a country with a really weak local currency you will have experienced the anxiety of local people to acquire pounds sterling, American dollars, Swiss francs – **any** hard currency unlikely to lose its value on the currency exchanges. Over a long period of time sterling has been a relatively stable currency and this has helped the UK to remain a prosperous country. It reflects the fact that goods and services produced here are saleable and in demand from the rest of the world and also that people come here in large numbers as visitors.

Activity 21

2 mins

Imagine that you live in a country that sells one major commodity to the UK as its main source of overseas income. It buys most of the manufactured goods it needs from the UK. The total trade in each direction is around £100 million and the current exchange rate is 1 local currency unit to £1.

The local currency then falls in value by 25%, due to a failure of another crop principally exported to other countries.

By how much would the country need to increase its exports to pay for the essential items it buys from the UK?

You will find the answer on page 119. It shows clearly the dire consequences which follow from a currency which falls in value.

If you work for an organization that imports or exports goods or services, then you will be aware how closely exchange rates are monitored. A small percentage movement in the rate can make a substantial difference to profits – or the difference between profit and loss.

7.3 Inflation

Inflation is often regarded with the same horror as cancer. Though this can be carried to extremes, there is no doubt that inflation, when it becomes rampant, can be a canker which blights the lives of millions of people.

■ Germany – 1920
  In Germany, after the end of the First World War in 1918, rampant inflation (often called hyper inflation) set in, largely caused by the unrealistic demands of the Allied powers with whom she had signed the Treaty of Versailles. The Mark collapsed, losing 50% of its value in **just one day** and became eventually worthless in a country which must import many essential products. The misery and despair which this caused to millions of people was a prime factor in the rise of Hitler and National Socialism in the 1920s and 1930s and ultimately of the Second World War.

■ Argentina – 2002

For some years, the Argentine currency had been pegged to the US dollar. In reality, it was worth far less, and eventually the underlying weakness of the Argentine economy made the link untenable. The economic realities have led to serious inflation, complete loss of confidence in the currency (at one time a new currency was introduced) and misery for Argentine citizens, with the threat of civil unrest constantly in the background.

These events, happening 80 years apart, illustrate the dangers of inflation which leads to the collapse of a currency. Many other examples could be quoted. Running a business becomes virtually impossible; a black market in 'hard' (i.e. trustworthy) currencies develops, and employees demand hugely increased wages to buy daily necessities whose prices are marked up daily, or sometimes hourly.

Though there have been periods of relatively steep inflation in the UK, most recently in the 1970s, this country has never experienced hyper inflation. The pound sterling has remained a relatively strong currency because of the underlying strength of the economy and a stable political system.

7.4 What causes inflation?

The Government assesses inflation by measuring the increase in cost of a 'basket' of standard shopping items and services over time. What goes into the basket is changed periodically to reflect our changing ways of life. Two measures are used, one including house price inflation and one excluding it. The figures are fed to the Bank of England Monetary Policy Committee each month as one of the main factors they consider when assessing the need for interest rate changes.

Nevertheless, there is continuing inflation here and many goods and services seem to move up inexorably in price, reflecting an imbalance between supply and demand.

Demand pull inflation

Demand pull inflation is what the ice cream vendor experienced on the local or 'micro' level. There were more people wishing to buy his product than he had product to sell. So, if he chose to put up his prices he could still sell his goods. On the global or 'macro' level, you can see the same effect when the supply of products like oil, which every country must have, is restricted.

Cost push inflation

The ice cream vendor's costs had not changed; he was simply increasing his price in response to increased demand.

But what if the price of ice cream, wafer biscuits, diesel fuel and road tax for his van should increase, for reasons outside his control? Then, he might eventually have to pass these costs on to his customers, simply to cover his own costs – regardless of the demand for his wares – and hope that they would still buy what is, whatever children may think, a non-essential product.

Labour-cost inflation

As you have already seen, wages, salaries, fees and so on are all ways of stating the price paid for the labour factor of production. Many trades and professions are labour intensive. The price of labour increases, the chances are that this will be passed on to consumers of goods and services and contribute to general inflation.

Trades unions that pursue successful claims are often identified with wage inflation, but non-unionized labour in occupations such as the law, sport, accountancy and politics also seek increases in payment. These can contribute to inflation, both directly and by influencing lower-paid people to seek increases on a 'me too' basis.

In the EU and other developed countries such as Australia, New Zealand, Canada and the USA, governments can contribute to labour-cost inflation by imposing 'on costs' (such as PAYE and NIC) on labour which rise steadily over the years.

It has often been said that there is no such thing as a free lunch; well there are no such things as free paid holidays, maternity leave, sick pay or time off for trade union activities.

Someone, usually the employer, has to pay, and this increases the total costs of labour. Sooner or later these costs will be passed on as higher prices, contributing to inflation.

Activity 22 ·
10 mins

S/NVQ B1.2, D1.1

Look at what your own organization pays for the main factors of production and raw materials which it uses. Take just **one** significant example of each, for example:

- rent paid for land used;
- direct labour costs;
- cost of a replacement machine;
- price of chief raw material.

Note down what has happened to the prices of each of these factors. Have they decreased, stayed the same or increased? If they have changed, by what percentage over the past year?

If the data is readily available, you will find it more informative to look at trends over a longer period, say three or more years.

_____

_____

_____

This activity should have shown clearly that it is easier to generalize about inflation than it is to gather evidence of it in a specific context. In reality, every individual and every organization has a unique inflation rate. The figures published in the media are generalized averages which are useful as a guide, but need to be adjusted to individual circumstances – as the following true incident shows.

A major company bought a chain of fish and chip shops. It did so at a time when its profits were high and so it agreed to pay a large sum for the goodwill of the business.

Within months of the acquisition, a serious drought caused the price of potatoes to double. Simultaneously restrictions on the amounts of cod and haddock which could be fished virtually doubled the price of its other main raw material.

In effect, this gave it a specific inflation rate of 100% on these items alone, costs which could not be passed on for fear of driving customers away to other forms of fast food.

Profitability slumped and the goodwill paid for began to look very expensive indeed.

In the USA, during the Great Depression of the 1930s, nearly 13 million people were unemployed, most of them with little or no access to welfare provision. In some developing countries in 2002 adult male unemployment is 50% or more of the available workforce.

Other individual organizations can suffer similar inflationary pressures, especially where they are dependent on particular raw materials, must rent desirable premises, have to replace capital equipment, or use specialist labour.

7.5 Unemployment

Unemployment is an unpalatable fact of economic life which has been alluded to frequently in this workbook. It is a scourge for many economies and a threat to the stability of their governments. It also creates anxiety, unhappiness and loss of self esteem for many of those who find themselves out of work through no fault of their own.

In cold, economic terms, labour is a factor of production which, like any other factor, has a market price. If its cost rises above what the labour market is prepared to pay, then some of the work it does may be taken over by machines (such as computers) the cost of which can be repaid in an acceptable time by savings in labour cost.

Alternatively, in the global economy, employers may simply look for lower total labour costs overseas. A phone call takes no longer to New Delhi, Kuala Lumpur or Beijing than it does to Manchester or Belfast. Some large bookmakers have moved telephone-based activities abroad, partially for reasons connected with taxation, but also to take advantage of lower labour costs.

Much of the unemployment in the UK stems from employers seeking to replace labour with capital, or to find cheaper unit costs of labour. But unemployment can also result from:

- the falling off, or collapse in demand for, specific activities, e.g. coal and milk delivery services are rare now that many people have central heating and buy milk from shops and supermarkets;
- the exhaustion of raw materials or the scrapping of a process that has become too expensive or unsafe – a fact which has closed many coal mines.

Activity 23 · 2 mins

Write down two examples each of the following causes of unemployment arising for reasons not directly concerned with the price of labour. Wherever possible, choose examples from your own experience.

Collapse in demand:

_____

_____

Exhaustion of raw materials:

_____

_____

Your answers could include a very large number of items, so it is possible only to quote a few generalized and well known examples here for you to compare them with.

Collapse in demand

Air travel has replaced ocean liners as the principal means of transporting passengers from continent to continent; central heating has replaced open fires as the chief way of heating most properties; asbestos has been replaced with other materials on health grounds; television has all but killed off many forms of live entertainment.

Exhaustion of raw materials

Many mines have run out of coal, or it has become too risky to continue mining, oil fields have run dry; much of the world's fisheries have disappeared through over fishing; some natural gas fields have already run out.

All of these matters, and any of those which you have listed, will have caused people's work to disappear. Some of them have caused enormous job losses, with profound social consequences for areas solely dependent upon them.

Of course, if suitable alternative employment is available, the effects are mitigated. But that is frequently difficult to find. If a whole area is dependent on a single occupation, such as textiles, mining, quarrying or steel-making, then it will be hard for redundant workers to find other jobs.

It would be a very brave government indeed which made full employment one of its manifesto commitments in the twenty-first century. There is no shortage of people on Earth, even if birth rates have declined in some developed countries. It becomes ever simpler to replace labour with capital as industrial robots and computer systems become ever more able to replicate human activity without becoming bored, dissatisfied or seeking higher pay or better conditions of service.

Self-assessment 1

30 mins

1 The three factors of production which every organization employs are:

_____

_____

_____

2 Suggest two reasons why organizations strive to become least cost producers in their fields.

_____

_____

3 Give one example each of:
a a situation where land has been created; and
b entrepreneurship that has discovered a profitable use for redundant or seemingly barren land.

a _____

b _____

4 Factors of production differ from _____ _____ in that

the latter are _____ in the process, whereas the former remain

_____ for further use.

5 Wheat, oil seed rape, tides and winds are all examples of _____ resources.

6 Which of the following represent non-renewable resources? Underline your selections.

solar power   natural gas   coal   timber
crude oil   iron ore   wool   sea fish

7 Other things being equal, the more _____ a factor of production

becomes, the _____ will be its _____ price.

8 If the cost of labour becomes relatively _____, organizations will

seek to _____ it with _____ equipment, or by finding

people prepared to _____.

9   Explain in your own words what you understand by the word 'monopoly'.

10 The following five sets of initials could relate to bodies which regulate formerly state-run industries. Three are genuine and two are not. Match the four regulatory bodies to the correct sets of initials.

OFFPITCH   OFWAT   OFGEM   OFFPISTE   OFTEL

Gas and electricity supply   Telecommunications   Water

11 What adverse effects can the use of subsidies have on the work of the price mechanism? Allowing for this, do you believe that there are circumstances where state subsidies can be justified?

_____

_____

_____

_____

12 Give two examples of indirect competition which could affect the activities of:

   ■ a bus operator in London, Manchester or Newcastle

_____

_____

   ■ a fish-and-chip shop

_____

_____

   ■ a cinema

_____

_____

13 The levying of _____ taxes, such as income tax and _____ tax, are examples of the government's _____ policies in action.

14 Indirect taxes, such as _____ and _____ are deemed to be _____ because they bear more heavily on people with _____ incomes.

15 Every government's dilemma concerning fiscal policy is that the electorate demand higher and higher levels of_____ _____, but are unwilling to see _____ rise to pay for them.

16 The letters MPC stand for the Bank of England's _____ _____ _____, which became independent of the government in 19_____.

17 Exchange rates measure the relative _____ power of two _____ and indicate the _____ strength of their economies.

18 Give one example each of:
   ■ cost push inflation;   _____
   ■ demand pull inflation;   _____
   ■ wage-related inflation.   _____

19 Unemployment can arise from causes such as the _____ of natural resources, the _____ of labour with _____ equipment, or the _____ of activities elsewhere in pursuit of _____ labour.

20 Uncontrolled or _____ inflation inevitably leads to _____ unemployment, which can _____ governments and lead to _____ gaining power.

8 Summary

- The economic and political decisions of governments affect every business and every individual in the community so everyone should take a close interest in them.

- Factors beyond governments' control, such as natural disasters and the decisions of multinational corporations, can have a profound effect on the economy in the short and longer term.

- The UK has a mixed economy in which central government retains responsibility for essential services such as health, but most goods and services are provided by privately run profit-seeking organizations.

- It is the price mechanism which keeps demand and supply in balance in a mixed economy.

- The global economy now allows and encourages businesses to move from one country, or continent, to another if the price of land, capital and labour exceeds levels which they are willing to pay. Manufacturing and administrative jobs are both affected by this trend.

- Subsidies, whether for political, social policy, or other reasons, distort the price mechanism and can cause problems to both providers and receivers in the longer term.

- Monopolistic practices, which also distort the price mechanism, are either banned or tightly controlled in the UK to prevent exploitation and profiteering.

- The government uses taxes (fiscal policy) and control of interest rates (monetary policy) to control inflationary trends.

- The government has no money of its own; it can spend only what the electorate is willing for it to raise through taxes.

- The dilemma of successive governments has been that electors desire better public services but resent paying taxes which provide the means of paying for them.

- In many countries rampant inflation has led to the collapse of currencies, unemployment on a vast scale, civil unrest and the election of extremist governments.

- Many laws stipulating what organizations can and cannot do have been enacted over centuries to protect the general public against the activities of unscrupulous businessmen.

- A stable economy, in which inflation is contained, the currency keeps its value and unemployment is the exception, provides the right climate for social stability and a democratic society. Only in such conditions can a government provide services such as health, state pensions, education and welfare, which have come to be accepted as the norm in the UK.

Session B
The global village

1 Introduction

Session A introduced the basic concepts and principles which define and underlie economic activities, almost regardless of how politicians and organizations try to influence them. You will find it very helpful to keep the basics in mind during this session, where the outlook widens to the world issues which influence all organizations here in the short, medium and long term.

The UK has long been a trading nation. Evidence of this is to be seen in countless ways. Here are just a few examples.

- Saffron cake is very popular in Cornwall. Saffron, a prized ingredient of Indian and Central Asian food, is thought to have been introduced to Cornwall by Phoenician traders perhaps hundreds of years B.C., who took tin from local mines back to their eastern Mediterranean lands.
- Dundee has been associated with marmalade for centuries. The Seville oranges from which it is made are almost exclusively imported to the UK. In World War Two special arrangements were made to secure supplies, as marmalade was believed important to maintaining morale.
- Before the Panama Canal was opened in 1914 linking the Atlantic and Pacific Oceans, sailing ships carried coal from ports in South Wales around the perilous Cape Horn, returning laden with guano from Chile. The guano, a fertilizer provided free by millions of sea birds, was used to fertilize arable farms here. The round trip under sail involved over 20,000 miles of peril and hardship.
- Flax grown in Northern Ireland's mild, moist climate was made into linen, then transformed into high quality fabrics and clothing for export throughout the world.

- In Norfolk and Suffolk the beautiful 'wool' churches are evidence of the medieval wool trade with continental Europe. Many of the weavers here were Huguenot refugees who had escaped from persecution in Europe.
- Joseph Banks, a scientist who sailed with the explorer Captain Cook in the eighteenth century, helped to found Kew Gardens, which was instrumental in transplanting rubber and tea to Malaysia and India respectively.
- Scottish malts are prized by connoisseurs of whisky. They have been an important source of foreign exchange for centuries, and remain so to this day.

2 The UK's international trade

2.1 Visible and invisible trade

The above examples illustrate the scope and variety of international trade to and from the UK. They can be divided into two categories for statistical purposes:

- 'visible';
- 'invisible'.

Visible items are products which have **tangible** (or physical) form. Examples we have discussed so far include imports of saffron, Seville oranges and guano, and exports of whisky, wool, coal, tin and clothing.

Invisible items are **intangible** (non-physical) and often take the form of a service or financial product. The invisible imports in the above illustrations included payments for services (the expertise of drainage engineers and weavers) and, for exports, expertise in railway construction and horticulture, which also brought longer-term benefits.

Activity 24 · 3 mins

List some other examples of visible and invisible trade, with as many as possible drawn from your own experience and that of your organization. Classify your examples into imports and exports and, wherever possible, give specific items rather than broad categories.

Imports		Exports	
Invisibles	**Visibles**	**Invisibles**	**Visibles**
1		1	
2		2	
3		3	
4		4	
5		5	

On page 119 you will find a completed grid, simply for comparison with your own.

You may have found that it was harder to think of individual examples of invisible items than of visible goods which the UK imports and exports.

Your lists could have included a huge variety of items. Selecting them should have helped get you into the right frame of mind for exploring the fascinating and complex issues of international trade and the global issues challenging the UK.

Mathematically, one billion is one **million** million, or 1,000,000,000,000. But in America, a billion is reckoned to be one **thousand** million, or 1,000,000,000. It makes quite a difference, whether you're measuring distances to the stars or trade deficits.

In this workbook one billion is taken to mean one thousand million (i.e. the American version), as this is used in all official figures such as the *Annual Abstract of Statistics*.

2.3 The balance of visible trade

Overall, in the year 2001, The UK:

- **exported** £ 191,000,000,000 of tangible goods – known as £191 billion by the American way of calculating one billion
- **imported** £224,000,000,000 of tangible goods – or £224 billion.

EXTENSION 2
A useful source of
statistics is the
Government's Annual
Abstract Of Statistics,
available from The
Stationery Office.

That left a **balance of trade** deficit of £33 billion – a vast sum to be in the red.

The figures are so enormous, and the process for collecting the data so prone to error, that it would be foolhardy to believe that they are precise. As you saw in Session A, the much quoted figure for inflation has to be viewed carefully, as in reality every individual and organization has a unique inflation rate.

Benjamin Disraeli, a nineteenth-century British Prime Minister, said:

'there are lies, damned lies and statistics'.

However, because the trade figures are so large, the chances are that there will be as many errors in one direction as another and many will probably cancel each other out, rather like the decisions of umpires and referees in sport. Players never seem to remember the times when they were fortunate. Over time good and bad decisions tend to cancel themselves out, if they are honestly made.

The trouble with official statistics is that politicians try to interpret them to prove that they are right and their opponents wrong. This can influence the way in which figures are collected and presented. But the sheer volume of figures is against their discrediting the figures entirely.

2.4 The balance on invisible items

Because of the size of the UK's balance of trade deficit in regard to visible earnings, its nett earnings from invisible items are extremely important. For many years, they more than compensated for the adverse trade gap between imports and exports of visible items.

In 2001, the UK had a surplus on the invisible items of £13,000,000,000, or £13 billion. This continues the pattern of many years, and reflects the UK's expertise in financial services and its popularity with tourists.

2.5 The balance of payments

The balance of payments brings together the figures for visible and invisible items to strike an overall balance each year – in simple terms not unlike a company profit and loss account. Bringing in the surplus on invisible items reduces the deficit on visible trade to an overall payments deficit of £20,000,000,000 – £20 billion – still a huge number.

EXTENSION 3
This extension summarizes some of the main figures from international trade, from which you will see how enormous the sums are. The statistical law of 'inertia of large numbers' states that large groups of data are more stable and reliable than small ones, so the figures should give a reasonably true picture.

2.6 Trends in balance of trade and balance of payments

In Extension 3 (pages 111–12) you will find the figures for the years 1997 to 2001 accumulated. They show that:

■ the total deficit on visible trade for five years was £123 billion;
■ the total balance of payments deficit for the same period was £63 billion.

2.7 The possible effects on the sterling exchange rate

Over a period of time the tendency for deficits to increase is worrying because it could put pressure on the value of the pound sterling. For the present, the deficit is being financed and virtually eliminated by other items, such as flows of investment capital. The relatively high interest rates maintained for several years by the Bank of England MPC have tended to maintain the exchange rate.

However, in the longer term it is essential for the UK to balance its books if it is to retain its prosperity and political influence in the world, just as any organization – public, private, or charitable – must.

The statistical data has been presented at the very start of this session because it shows clearly how vital international trade is to the UK economy. Since the whole of the session is concerned with European and international issues, it is as well to have a picture of the colossal figures involved in the UK's trade from the outset.

More detail will be added as the session progresses, providing you with breakdowns of the total figures to show clearly:

■ what we export and to whom;
■ what we import and from where.

The following activity asks you to concentrate on imports and exports as they affect your own organization.

Activity 25 · 30 mins

S/NVQ B1.2, D1.1

This Activity may provide the basis of appropriate evidence for your S/NVQ portfolio. If you are intending to take this course of action, it might be better to write your answers on separate sheets of paper.

Using either a separate sheet of paper or the table provided below, make a list of:

■ the top five items that your organization imports and from where, including, if possible, an indication of their volume and value in pounds sterling

■ the top five items which your organization exports, the chief destinations for them and their volume and value in pounds sterling.

Remember that, so far as imports and exports are concerned:

■ buying services such as shipping, air travel and tourist facilities from overseas providers is just as much an import as buying materials such as paper pulp, raw sugar, aluminium or oil;

■ conversely, selling services such as hotel accommodation and insurance to foreign visitors is an export, just as is selling paper, refined sugar and aluminium or petroleum products overseas.

An example has been given as the first item in the table.

	IMPORTS			EXPORTS	
Material/ Service	Country of origin	Volume/ Value in £ sterling	Material/ Service	Destination	Volume/ Value in £ sterling
Wood pulp	Norway	50,000 tons/ £5 million	Fine papers/ Stationery	EU countries	5,000 tons/ £1.5 million
1					
2					
3					
4					
5					

If you believed that your organization is not involved in exporting and importing, you may have received some surprises by doing this activity. For example:

- if an NHS hospital treats overseas patients who pay for the services directly, or through a health insurance scheme, that will count as an export;
- the same hospital may source drugs from foreign countries, which are imports;
- a call centre may buy equipment from overseas, which is an import, but sell insurance services by phone to foreign buyers, which then count as exports;
- a department store may import large quantities of goods from around the world and resell some of them, together with UK-produced items to foreign tourists, which represent exports.

The effect of exchange rates on organizations

In Activity 25, in the example given in the first line of the table, the hypothetical company imports £5 millions' worth of wood pulp and exports £1.5 millions' worth of paper products, selling the remainder of its output in the UK. So the organization has a personal balance of trade deficit of £3.5 million.

Now, visualize a fall in the value of sterling of 5%, so that each £1 is worth only 95 pence.

The cost of imported pulp will now be ($100/95 \times 5,000,000$) or £5,263,158 – over a quarter of a million pounds more, because each £1 buys 5% less.

The value of the exports will now be ($95/100 \times 1,500,000$) or £1,425,000 – a fall of £75,000 in value because the overseas importer needs to spend only 95% of the former cost to buy the same amount of pounds to pay for the goods.

Five per cent is a very significant loss of value for a currency, especially if it happens rapidly. But it is trivial compared with the falls which have happened in countries such as Germany and Argentina, described in Session A, or in Italy, France, Brazil and Turkey. You may have visited countries where it has happened and seen at first hand the anxiety and near panic which it can cause.

In the example, the company is both importing and exporting. It is adding value to its exports and selling finished products for three times the cost of the imported raw materials – £300 per ton as compared with £100 per ton.

Many organizations of course do just that; most things in economics are not straightforward.

An organization which imports raw materials, processes them and sells on the finished goods will have to run faster to stay where it is by either selling more as the currency value depreciates, or by increasing prices, if the market will bear it. But, as you have seen in Session A, competition and the price mechanism may not allow it to do so.

If you are solely an importer, say of American wines, then you may find that your entire business is badly hit by a fall in the value of sterling, which you are powerless to influence. Conversely, if you are an exporter, you may find that an increase in value of sterling will hit your sales, as your customers find it more expensive to buy pounds to pay you with.

In 2000, 21% of UK household income came from payments made by the State. This is an increase of more than 10% over 15 years under succeeding Conservative and Labour Governments. Such spending, however desirable it may be, can only be afforded by a financially sound economy.

Activity 25 will have given you a picture of how your own organization may be affected by movements in exchange rates. Unless it uses no imported goods or services (which is unlikely given that the UK imports now exceed £200 billion per year) and is without export earnings (more likely, but exports averaged £175 billion over the years 1997 to 2001), then movements in exchange rates will have a very significant effect – for good or ill.

The UK has avoided catastrophic falls in the value of sterling, but the upward trend in balance of payments deficits must raise long-term concerns about it and the prosperity which goes with a stable currency in which people throughout the world have confidence.

The answer is, as always, for an island nation not self sufficient in resources, and dependent on the skills and ingenuity of its people:

- to export relatively more;
- to import relatively less;
- to remain outward looking and aware that, in the medium to long term, you can't spend what you don't earn.

3 The UK's trading partners

The simplest and quickest way to see with whom the UK trades is to open a world atlas. Look at the overall projection of the world and the six continents inhabited by several billion potential customers and suppliers. There is hardly a place on earth that has no trade links with this country.

3.1 The United Nations (UN)

At the beginning of 2003, the UN has 191 member states and it would be hard to find any that the UK does not trade with, short of embargoes or insurmountable tariff barriers being imposed.

3.2 The British Commonwealth

There are more than 50 Commonwealth countries with whom the UK has close political, trading and cultural links. They include wealthy, developed nations such as Australia and Canada on the one hand and some of the world's poorest countries, for example, Sierra Leone, on the other. Trade with the UK is vital to the poorer countries, which may depend on exports of commodities such as bananas, cocoa, coffee, copper or iron ore, and cane sugar.

3.3 The United States of America (USA)

The USA has a land area of more than 9 million square kilometres and a population in 2002 estimated at 276 million – just over 30 people per square kilometre. By comparison, the area of Europe, including European Russia, is 10 million square kilometres and its population is estimated at more than 700 million – 70 people per square kilometre. The area of the UK is 244 square kilometres and its population is nearly 60 million – 245 people per square kilometre.

The USA has the world's largest single economy and is the dominant power in world economics and politics. Many multinational companies are based there and many of the technologies that affect farming, pharmaceuticals and other activities throughout the world have been developed there.

With the demise of the USSR as a true world power, following the near collapse of its centrally directed economy and division into many individual states, the USA is the only true super power left at present.

The USA has enormous economic advantages. The next activity invites you to suggest what they may be.

Activity 26 · 3 mins

List up to five economic factors which you believe the USA has in its favour compared with European countries. Think in terms of factors of production – land, labour, capital and natural resources to guide your selections.

You will find some suggestions against which to compare your own in Extension 4. They are so numerous that it is not surprising that the US is so dominant in world affairs.

EXTENSION 4
This extension comprises a brief survey of the USA's intrinsic economic advantages.

The USA rouses strong emotions concerning its economic, foreign and defence policies. The activities of multinationals, ranging from Walt Disney to Exxon, from McDonalds to Monsanto, Microsoft and the communications giant AOL Time Warner, penetrate everywhere on earth.

Whatever views other countries may hold about the USA, it would be a grave mistake to ignore it. Every country in the world will continue to be affected by the policies framed in Washington and the industrial and commercial power houses of California, Detroit, Chicago, New York and Seattle.

The information given here about the European Union is based on the actual membership of 15 states in December 2002. Another ten countries have been accepted for membership, but are not yet full members. They are Cyprus, Czech Republic, Estonia, Hungary, Latvia, Lithuania, Malta, Poland, Slovakia, Slovenia. Following the formal admission of these countries to full membership by June 2004, talks about membership are planned to re-start with Turkey.

The USA continues to be the UK's largest single trading partner, despite the 3,000 miles of Atlantic Ocean which divide the two countries (compared with 22 miles of English Channel between England and France). This shows how strong the necessity is to trade with such a giant economic power, which was also our ally in two world wars. Analysis of the remaining EU countries would show that they too have strong trading links across the Atlantic, however great the political gulf may be.

3.4 The European Union (EU)

The EU already comprises 15 European states, some of them very large economies in their own right, including our own and those of Germany, France and Italy.

Activity 27 · 3 mins

From the following list of European countries, select the six which are **already** members (not just potential members) of the EU by underlining your choices.

Sweden	Slovenia	Monaco	Denmark
Spain	Luxembourg	Latvia	Greece
Liechtenstein	Norway	Portugal	Lithuania

EXTENSION 5
Extension 5 gives a full list of actual EU member states and an indication of some potential new members.

In fact, the Treaty of Nice states that **any** European State which has a democratic system of government may join, so there can be no definitive list.

In Extension 5, you will find a complete list of current members. There is also an indication of those states which may wish to join in the future. The EU, one of the most powerful groups of trading nations on earth, will be examined in detail in section 4 of this session.

3.4 Other major nations and continents with whom we trade

Other partners with whom the UK trades include:

The former USSR has split into many states, including many which are economically underdeveloped and often beset by border disputes and even civil war. The former USSR republics include: Azerbaijan; Belarus; Dagestan; Georgia; Chechnya; Armenia; Ukraine; Uzbekistan; Turkmenistan; Kyrgystan and Kazakhstan.

■ Russia and the former USSR satellite republics in Asia, with economies currently in various states of development following the rapid demise of centralized communist power in the 1980s and 1990s;

■ the oil exporting countries of the Middle East, crucial to the world economy and currently highly dependent on a single commodity for their prosperity;

■ China, the most populous country on earth, which now includes Hong Kong and which is keen to expand trade with western nations;

■ South America, with the huge countries of Mexico, Brazil, Chile and Argentina; having vast resources on the one hand and grinding poverty on the other;

■ Japan and the so-called Pacific rim countries such as South Korea and Taiwan which are emerging as major manufacturing countries.

The UK's worst imbalance of trade is with Japan, a country which relies on ingenuity and manufacturing expertise and has few natural resources of its own. Together with China and the Pacific rim countries, Japan accounts for

£17.6 billion – well over half – of our enormous £30 billion deficit on visible trade in 2000 – a proportion which is almost certainly increasing.

In Extension 3, you will find a table summarizing all of the UK's visible trade with the whole world. The figures are broken down:

- firstly by the broad categories of goods which we import and export;
- secondly to show our largest trading partners and the individual balance of trade surpluses or deficits which we have with them.

Few Commonwealth countries are specifically listed in the table. Most appear in the Other countries category, with whom collectively the UK has a £10 billion trade deficit.

> The UK's balance of visible trade deficit is larger than many developing countries' total outputs of goods and services.

It is important to remember that, although in UK trade terms imports and exports from countries like Nigeria, Zambia, Guyana, Sri Lanka and other Commonwealth countries may be relatively small, our imports from them may be a major source of local employment and foreign exchange – or simply survival.

Other European countries – France, Spain, Portugal and Belgium in particular – have strong historical and commercial links to former colonies throughout the world and a long history of reciprocal trading with them, often vital to local economies.

To complete the next activity, you will need to study the figures provided in Extension 3. They may contain some surprises.

Activity 28 · 10 mins

> The economy of California alone is reckoned to be among the largest in the world, even though at the start of 2003 it was technically bankrupt! It is as big as the economies of some countries. California has an area of more than 400,000 square kilometres and a population of nearly 34 million.

Study Table (c) in Extension 3, then write down:

1   with which country we have the largest trade **deficit** and how large it is

_____

2   with which country we have the largest trade **surplus** and how great the surplus is

_____

3   taking the far eastern countries of China, Hong Kong, South Korea and Taiwan, the total deficit that the UK has with them

4   the total you arrived at in question 3 as a percentage of the total UK deficit of £30 billion

5   with which countries the UK's trade is in balance, i.e. having a surplus or deficit of less than £1 billion

6   the largest **single** trading partner which the UK has and the total of the import and export trade with it

The answers can be found on pages 119–20.

3.5 The world's sole economic super power

The answer to the last question in Activity 28 once again shows how important the UK's trading relationship with the USA is, a fact which would be true for a high percentage of all the UN's 191 member states.

The next section looks more closely at the EU and its institutions, which are of vital importance to the UK and its well being. However, this section has shown clearly that global issues are equally important in the long term and that the economic dominance of the USA cannot be ignored.

Just before we turn to European matters, the following true case study illustrates just how ramified trading patterns now are.

> The IKEA furniture company is based in Almhult, a small town, 300 miles from Stockholm in Sweden. From small beginnings it has grown into a business with 170 stores and 70,000 employees in many countries. Its annual turnover now approaches 10 billion euros, or £6.5 billion. Some other statistics are as follows:

- its headquarters are in Sweden, which is a member of the EU;
- the store with the largest individual turnover is in London, exceeding £130 million annually;
- Germany produces the highest sales in total for an individual country;
- it uses approximately 2,000 suppliers in 55 countries, including the 15 EU members;
- the principal suppliers are in Sweden itself – and China whose trade with western nations is, as you have seen from the UK figures, of growing significance.

Activity 29

3 mins

Look at the IKEA case study and say how you expect that the company's activities might affect:

- the UK's balance of visible trade with Sweden;
- Germany's balance of visible trade with Sweden;
- UK exports of visible trade items;
- Sweden's balance of visible trade with China;
- the exchange rate of sterling against the Swedish Krona.

_____

_____

_____

_____

_____

You will find the answers on page 120.

As with most questions on trade and economics, there are no definitive answers of the 2+2 = 4 variety. Other factors also come into it, such as the possible creation of retail and manufacturing jobs in the UK, which you were not asked to consider.

The IKEA company will probably be known to many readers, either as customers or perhaps through working for one of their 2,000 suppliers. Though the company is very large by normal standards, the effect which it will have **individually** on international trade and exchange rates is limited.

However, when you add up the activities of such companies – and the much larger ones in petrochemicals, vehicle manufacturing, pharmaceuticals, agriculture – then the decisions of private organizations begin to have a really significant effect on whole economies, and may be taken independently of any political or social concerns of national governments.

4 The European Union (EU)

4.1 A brief history 1952 – 2002

The European Coal & Steel Community (ECSC) was formed in 1952 and consisted of France, Germany, Holland, Italy, Luxembourg and Belgium – countries which had all suffered dreadfully from the wars which ravaged Europe over the centuries.

The original impetus for the formation of a European trading bloc was the desire to rescue Europe from a seemingly endless round of wars and prohibitive expenditure on defence.

France and Germany had been at war in 1870, 1914 and again in 1939. Even between the two World Wars, there had been an invasion of part of Germany by France, and a history of mistrust and hatred prevailed which seemed to have no end.

Italy, like Germany, had been governed by a brutal dictatorship between the World Wars. It had been allied to Hitler's Germany and eventually suffered a crushing defeat and the ruination of much of its industrial base and historic heritage.

Ypres, a beautiful city in Belgium, is associated forever with the unimaginable horrors of trench warfare and mindless waste of life in World War One rather than the splendour of its medieval cloth hall and its dedication to trade.

During World War Two millions of people died in throughout Europe, and appalling destruction was wrought on historic cities, towns and buildings from Berlin to Antwerp and from St. Malo to Rotterdam.

In 1955, the 'group of six', as the original member states of the EU became known, agreed to establish a wider common market in goods, services and people. Two years later the Treaty of Rome gave legal effect to the European Economic Community, or EEC, which came into being in 1958.

Since then, the Community has widened until it now includes the 15 member states listed in Extension 5. The UK joined following a referendum in 1973. The UK was initially reluctant to become involved in what was perceived by most leaders here as the beginning of some kind of potential European super state.

There were concerns here about the potential effects on Commonwealth nations with whom the UK had long histories of mutual assistance – including during time of war – and on the special relationship with the USA which had twice intervened to assist this country during the two World Wars.

The UK had not been invaded or defeated in either war. It had suffered considerable loss of life, and destruction of much of its historic heritage in many towns and cities through aerial bombardments by the German Luftwaffe's aircraft and V1 and V2 rockets.

Furthermore, the British constitution, systems of government and law were very different to their European counterparts and had evolved separately over nearly a thousand years.

4.2 What has impeded the EU's inception and growth?

The present 15 members of the EU have a population of 379 million in a land area of 3,250,000 square kilometres, or 116 people per square kilometre. By comparison the USA has 276 million in a land area of 9,363,000 square kilometres – or just over 30 people per square kilometre.

Extension 4 summarizes the economic advantages which the USA enjoys. It is plain by comparison that European countries do not enjoy many of them.

■ Europe is densely populated by comparison with the USA.

■ Its many land borders have been the subject of bloody wars for centuries and there was a potential threat from the East as the 'iron curtain' descended between Russia and Western Europe after 1945.

■ Its peoples, though ingenious, enterprising and imaginative, have many languages, diverse cultures, mutual distrusts and plain mutual dislikes after centuries of warfare.

■ Until recently there was no common currency, with the result that there were many costs and barriers to trade and some currencies were much stronger than others. Even now, not all European countries have adopted the euro.

■ There are customs and tariff barriers between some European states, many of which have smaller economies than individual American states such as California or Texas.

■ Much of the European capital base and infrastructure were in ruins in 1945, but America's was unscathed and actually developed, driven by war manufactures.

■ America is rich in natural resources whereas in Europe they are either lacking – Ireland lacks coal and oil reserves – or are being rapidly depleted – Germany has used up its near-surface coal deposits and must mine deeply to obtain coal. Germany has very little oil.

■ The climate in much of northern Europe is harsh and hostile to the growing of many staple crops.

The EU's founding fathers, (Adenauer in Germany, Schumann and Monnet in France, Spaak in Holland and de Gasperi in Italy) all had first-hand experience of the horrors of total warfare. Germany was divided and its eastern portion would continue to be a satellite of Russia until 1990.

While the geographical, historical and climatic conditions that have held Europe back cannot be changed, there are certain things that could be copied from across the Atlantic such as:

■ political stability;
■ freedom of movement for goods and people;
■ a single strong currency and legal system.

It is impossible to separate clearly the political and economic motivating factors which have driven the subsequent growth of the EU, and which have taken it from the original group of six to 15 members, with the possibility of extension to 20 or more in the foreseeable future.

Throughout history, many wars have been fought for economic reasons, and continue to be into the twenty-first century. Usually, disputes arise over border areas, just as many people individually fall out with their neighbours.

Making European countries so mutually dependent economically that war becomes inconceivable is surely the best way of avoiding future conflagrations.

4.3 UK trade with EU countries

Collectively, the UK does over half its total trade with the other EU member states:

■ £108 billion of our exports go to the EU out of £188 billion total world exports;
■ £111 billion of our imports come from the EU out of a world total of £218 billion.

These are huge numbers and it is well to bear in mind Disraeli's warning about statistics. For example, some goods shipped via European ports to destinations outside the EU may be counted as exports directly to EU states. Overall, this could increase the visible trade deficit with the EU to a figure much greater than the £3 billion suggested – and increase the figure for exports to other countries by more than £10 billion.

The problem with all statistics that have political implications is that politicians try to present them in a way that supports their own objectives. So, for example:

■ a pro-Europe British politician will wish to stress the value of UK trade with the EU, whereas
■ a Eurosceptic will wish to emphasize the UK's trade beyond Europe.

What both of them should accept is that trade with the European mainland is vital to the UK's continuing prosperity. A stable, peaceful Europe is vital to the UK's national interests.

Activity 30

Using the data shown in Extension 3, rank the EU states in order, from most favourable balance of visible trade with the UK to least favourable balance.

Include in your list all the other countries of the EU whose individual trade figures are not listed because their trade with the UK is below £1 billion per annum.

_____

_____

_____

_____

_____

_____

_____

You will find confirmation of your rankings and the missing countries on page 120.

4.4 The Eurozone

The American economy illustrates the value of a single currency. In the USA the dollar is in use among 276 million people across a federation of 50 states. In addition, it is used as both a trading and a reserve currency throughout the world.

The Roman Empire, which lasted for centuries, also used a single currency – from North Africa to Northern Europe.

From January 2002 most European currencies, including the German Mark, began to be replaced with a single currency. The euro is now used by more than 300 million people, though by 2002 it had still not established itself as an international benchmark currency to rival the dollar.

Only Sweden, Denmark and the UK are still outside this 'Eurozone'. The Danish electorate voted against joining in a referendum held in 2000; the UK government has yet to hold such a referendum. The UK government has announced a series of economic tests which must be passed before the choice of whether or not to join is put to a referendum in England, Northern Ireland, Scotland and Wales at an unspecified date.

Once again, it is impossible to distinguish between the political, cultural and economic considerations which have influenced the views of those countries which adopted the euro and those, Sweden, Denmark and the UK, which did not. There is probably greater suspicion of the motives underlying moves towards monetary union in these countries than in the other states of Europe. There is also perhaps more long-term confidence in sterling than there was in the franc or the lira, both of which at some time suffered catastrophic falls in value during the twentieth century. Sterling has never collapsed, although it has depreciated significantly against the dollar over a period of many years (which has included two costly wars).

As this workbook is concerned chiefly with the UK (which is not a member of the Eurozone), this section will not be extended into the realms of speculation regarding the euro. For the present, the UK has been outside the Eurozone and has been since its inception in 1999, during which period trade with Europe and the world generally has continued. Neither has Denmark's refusal to join prevented its membership of the EU from continuing. In the meantime the euro, after losing value after its launch, has stabilized and taken its place on the European economic scene with very few teething problems, though there were suspicions in several countries that the changeover was used to hide price increases.

4.5 The EU's key institutions

The Council of Ministers

The Council of Ministers is the key decision-making body in the EU and comprises one minister drawn from each of the member countries, regardless of its size or economic stature. The UK government's key representative is normally the Foreign Secretary, although other ministers will attend certain meetings instead, according to the topic being discussed. The Council is normally chaired by each EU country in turn, for a six-month period.

The Council is not in permanent session, as a national government would be, but meets on an ad hoc basis. Although the ministers are nominated to the

Council by their own governments rather than being elected to it directly, they have been elected in their own countries as members of their own parliaments.

The European Commission

In effect, the Commission is equivalent to the Civil Service in the UK. It consists of a number of Commissioners appointed by member states for a four-year term which is renewable. Commissioners are not elected and most of them are former politicians. The Commission has a president, who normally holds the office for four years before being replaced by someone of a different nationality.

Since 1958 there has been one German president, one Belgian, two Italian, two French, one from the UK, one from the Netherlands and two from Luxembourg. Given that Luxembourg is by far the smallest EU State, this is an indication of the difficulty which member states have in agreeing a choice from one of the larger countries, such as Spain.

The Commissioners are pledged to take a Europe-wide view of issues and not to represent simply their own country's interests.

The Commission has several functions:

- to make proposals on recommended courses of action to the Council of Ministers
- to implement the decisions of the Council
- to promote the EU's interests in defined ways.

The Commissioners are supported in Brussels by a large bureaucracy, which does research into areas of potential interest to the EU and assists with implementing and monitoring decisions taken.

The European Parliament

This is the only EU body whose members are elected **directly** by their own constituents in their own countries, though the constituency boundaries are much wider than those of the national ones. They are now elected by proportional representation.

The UK has 87 Members of the European Parliament (MEPs), as compared with 659 MPs elected to Westminster.

In June 1999 the first elections involving proportional representation were held. London became one constituency rather than ten, represented collectively by a number of MEPs.

The Parliament can dismiss the Commissioners and has some powers over the way in which the vast EU budget is spent.

The European Court of Justice

This European Court of Justice is responsible for applying European Treaties and interpreting and adjudicating on disputes which may arise. The judges' decisions are binding on each member state, taking precedence over decisions made in its own courts. As such, they are a continuing source of friction between the Court in Luxembourg and EU Governments.

(Note that the European Court of Justice is a totally different court from the European Court of Human Rights – which is not an EU institution.)

Activity 31

S/NVQ DI.I

This Activity may provide the basis of appropriate evidence for your S/NVQ portfolio. If you are intending to take this course of action, it might be better to write your answers on separate sheets of paper.

Note down:

1 The name of the MEPs who represent the European constituency in which you currently work.

_____

2 Any particular interests which any of them represent in the European Parliament, and any which are of particular relevance to your own organization.

_____

_____

3 The region of that constituency, i.e. the geographical areas which it contains, for example, the counties and its approximate population

_____

_____

4 The average number of people (**not** voters) across the UK which each MEP represents by comparison with the average represented by a Westminster MP (assume the UK's population is 60 million)

_____

_____

5 Which present members of the EU have not had a President of the Commission?

_____

_____

You will find the answers on page 121.

Unless you are quite exceptional, you will have had to do some research through your colleagues, the public library or the Internet for this activity. The average number of people represented by an MEP is over 7.5 times that represented by a Westminster MP, whose average constituencies in the UK have 91,000 voters.

MEPs are the only people elected directly to any EU institution, but their elections provoke little interest and very low voter turnouts. Yet they are the only people – as a body – who have any power over the way in which the colossal budgets are spent, and they have ultimate power to dismiss the Commission.

In fact, that power is a blunt instrument. MEPs can dismiss the Commission only as a total body, not an individual Commissioner who has transgressed. This has come close to happening once, in 2000, because of objections to the way in which some Commissioners were behaving. It led to a continuing enquiry into possible corruption and malpractice within the Commission.

The EU Budget and the Common Agricultural Policy (CAP)

The Commission's budgetary figures for 2002 show that the EU budget will total £63.7 billion, equivalent to one third of the UK's total visible exports. This money is contributed by the 15 member states and spent for agreed purposes through the Commission's administration.

In 2000, the most recent year for which all the figures are available, the income and expenditure looked like this.

Country	Contribution in 2000		Application of money	Spending in 2000	
	%	£ billion		%	£ billion
Germany	25%	14.1	CAP	45%	26.5
France	16%	9.4	Regional aid	35%	18.9
UK	16%	9.0	Foreign aid	8%	4.8
Italy	12%	7.1	Admin	5%	3.0
Spain	7%	4.2	Research	4%	2.3
Netherlands	6%	3.6	Other	3%	1.4
Belgium	4%	2.2			
Remaining 8 States	14%	7.3			
TOTALS	100%	56.9		100%	56.9

Forty-five percent of the budget (£26.5 billion) was spent on the CAP in 2000, which is a lower proportion than in some previous years.

Fifty years earlier, the CAP was born out of food shortages in post-war Europe and memories of near-starvation in World War Two. The intention was to achieve self sufficiency in food production for the original six member states, an objective which was achieved.

However, other aspects of the policy, such as the imposition of tariffs on non-EU countries and the creation of vast surpluses in the 1980s, have made it the most contentious aspect of EU policy, and successive Commissions and Councils of Ministers have said that they will reform it.

4.6 Does any of this matter to the UK?

You are recommended to look at broadsheet newspapers such as *The Times*, *The Guardian*, *The Daily Telegraph*, *The Independent*, *The Scotsman*, *The Herald* (Glasgow), *The Press and Journal* (Aberdeen), *The Western Mail* and *The Financial Times* or their Sunday equivalents, on a regular basis – and to listen to BBC Radio 4 or World Service broadcasts which provide regular, authoritative and approachable accounts of the EU and world affairs.

The way in which the EU's budget is funded and spent certainly matter to the UK.

Just as the UK government has no money other than what its citizens are willing to pay in taxes, so the EU has no money other than what member states are prepared to contribute.

The table above shows clearly that Germany, at £14 billion, is by far the largest contributor to the total budget and that the UK is third, at around £9 billion.

A cursory glance at the tabloid press or at the schedules of popular television and radio stations would suggest that none of this had any bearing on life here. But the activities of the EU's institutions and political direction **do** affect everyone's lives here in many ways.

The broadsheet newspapers and in particular Radio 4, report regularly and often in depth both what is happening and what might happen. They often do so in approachable ways, reasonably free of economists' jargon and are an excellent way of keeping abreast of events, though you must allow for the fact that no one is completely unbiased in the way they interpret the facts they report.

Looking at papers from different parts of the political spectrum will help to balance up the opinions given on the facts reported – and allow you to develop your own informed view.

The aspects of life in the UK which decisions taken by European institutions can affect include:

- hours of work and general working conditions;
- price of food and how it is to be produced;
- food hygiene;
- employment law;
- standards applied to health and safety;
- environmental law;
- quotas for fisheries;
- weights and measures;
- immigration and emigration to and from the UK;
- the overall shape of farming and the nature of the countryside.

All these matters can affect employment, the cost of living and the quality of life here. The UK has around a sixth of the total present EU population – 60 million out of 380 millions. That, plus its economic strengths and influence in the world, demand that its collective voice should be heard, based on rational opinions formed by as many as possible of the electorate here.

4.7 Is there economic life in Europe beyond the EU?

Many pro-Europeans would say that it is impossible to survive outside the EU, while opponents argue that the UK could get along very well on its own. So, apart from the former communist bloc countries, are there any European countries which have chosen not to seek membership of the EU? And how are they doing?

Activity 32 · 3 mins

By the terms of the Treaty of Nice, 2000, it is open to any European state which can prove that it is democratically governed to apply for membership of the EU.

Write down the names of two or three Western European Democracies which have not applied for membership of the EU.

_____

_____

The answer is given on page 121.

Mention has already been made of the possible enlargement of the EU to include former communist countries.

There are strong arguments for and against such expansion, as the following case study shows.

> In 2002, Poland is a candidate state expecting to join the EU. It has an area of more than 300,000 square kilometres, 38.5 million people, decrepit heavy industries and a vast number of small farmers. Unemployment in 2002 was 17% of the adult workforce, compared with 8.5% within the Eurozone as a whole.

This was the view from inside the EU.

■ Some existing members of the EU were concerned that extension of CAP subsidies to Polish farmers could be prohibitively expensive. They therefore advocated providing subsidies at a lower rate.

■ The problems which West Germany has experienced for more than 10 years in re-absorbing former East Germany made some countries nervous of embracing another large country – where would the money come from?

■ The prospect of extending further aid to a populous country, whose people would be nett beneficiaries, perhaps for decades, did not thrill everyone.

This was the view within Poland itself.

It is one of the supreme ironies of history that the final trigger for World War Two was the Nazi invasion of Poland. When Germany was eventually defeated, Poland fell under the effective control of Communist Russia for more than 40 years following the savageries of Hitler's occupation.

■ Many Polish people were fearful that their small farmers would be thrown out of work when large agri-businesses moved in, substituting capital equipment for labour. Similar effects could be caused by hypermarkets and supermarkets taking business from small shops – and from farmers too, if they chose to import produce from more capital-intensive farms elsewhere in the world.

■ Many Poles feared for the future of the Roman Catholic religion and the spread of a secular society with lower moral standards than they believed they had. The Polish-born Pope was drawn into the argument in this largely Roman Catholic country.

■ The Polish government had already embarked on a programme of agricultural reform, which many people believe gives an ominous foretaste of things to come.

■ Both the Polish government and Polish farmers were angry that EU farm subsidies under the CAP might be paid to them at a much lower rate than for existing EU members.

4.8 The EU 50 years on

At the 2002 Earth Summit in August 2002 in Johannesburg, South Africa, 60,000 delegates from virtually all UN member countries, gathered to discuss:

■ the world's environment and climatic changes;
■ the gap between the world's rich and poor nations.

Many of the issues raised affect, or could affect, every organization in the UK and the EU – whatever happens as a result of the Summit itself.

One of the primary purposes of the European Coal and Steel Community (ECSC), which preceded the EU, was to put an end to the wars which had ravaged the continent for centuries. Today, descendants of the founding fathers of the ECSC can reasonably claim that:

■ by 2002 there have been 50 years without a general European war since the foundations of the present EU were laid in 1952;

Whatever the economic and political arguments about the future of Europe, this must surely stand as a great achievement which has brought enormous economic and political benefits in Europe and beyond.

5 International organizations which influence the UK

5.1 The World Bank

The World Bank comprises the International Bank for Reconstruction and Development (IBRD) and the International Development Association (IDA). It was founded in 1945 when major cities, including Tokyo, London, Berlin, Rotterdam, Belgrade, Warsaw, Leningrad, Antwerp, Hamburg and countless others were in ruins after six years of total war. At that time, the need for reconstruction and development cried out from every newspaper, every radio broadcast, cinema newsreel and – for the privileged few – from the new fangled invention of television.

The IBRD's present function is primarily to assist developing countries. Loans are made on a reasonably commercial basis. The Bank will assess each project proposed – perhaps a hydro electric scheme or the development of a new port – and assure itself that the investment will yield a return sufficient to pay interest and, over time, the capital advanced as well. The profits are used to fund developmental projects.

In 1998 the World Bank advanced around £7 billion nett to developing countries, compared with £26.5 billion spent on the CAP.

Desirable schemes which are not designed to yield commercial returns can be financed by the IDA, the other part of the World Bank.

The IDA takes a less commercial view than the IBRD. For example, it may provide money for educational and agricultural projects for which the short-term benefits are less certain, but which may produce great long-term ones to countries too poor to fund them.

5.2 The International Monetary Fund (IMF)

Like the World Bank, the IMF was founded in 1945. Its purpose was to encourage the expansion of world trade and make loans to countries to help them overcome balance of payments difficulties which, if uncorrected, would threaten their currency. The aim was to avoid the catastrophic collapses in the value of currencies which are frequently linked to political turmoil, the onset of dictatorial rule and potentially to the outbreak of war.

While this has helped many states, including the UK, to overcome difficulties, the conditions which the IMF attaches to loans and its power to affect a country's internal affairs often cause controversy.

Brazil, Argentina's northern neighbour, the largest country in South America and one of the world's ten largest economies, has experienced similar problems leading to a fall of more than 20% in the exchange rate of the Brazilian currency, the real, against the dollar.

In August 2001 the IMF lent $8 billion to the Argentine government to help it make loan repayments which would otherwise have been beyond its capacity. The IMF attached conditions to the loan which it deemed some months later had not been met. It therefore refused to pay the December instalment. The country was plunged into crisis, with foreign debts totalling $141 billion and adult unemployment standing at 18%. The peso was devalued a few weeks later by 30%. The President declared Argentina bankrupt – in other words, unable to meet its international debts. Emergency financial measures imposed by the government led to rioting and the threat of political instability.

5.3 What has this to do with the UK and its business organizations?

You may well ask what this has to do with the organization for which you work. After all, these events were occurring thousands of miles away.

That's true, but it has happened here too. In 1967 the UK was forced to devalue the pound from a fixed value of $2.80 to $2.40 (around 8.5%) as a condition imposed by the IMF for continuing assistance to the UK economy. The pound was over-valued and did not truly reflect what it would purchase from countries which were using strong currencies such as the Swiss franc, the Japanese yen or the dollar.

The Prime Minister at the time, Harold Wilson, announced on television that 'the £ in your pocket is worth the same as before'.

Was he right in 1967 and, if so, does the same apply to the Argentinean peso or the Brazilian real? The following activity will help you decide.

Activity 33 ·   8 mins

Imagine three different Argentinean businesses:

- a company which exports 5 million pesos' worth of wine to the UK;
- a company which imports North Sea Oil worth 20 million pesos;
- A market trader who buys produce locally and sells it via market stalls in Rio de Janeiro. He buys 75,000 pesos' worth each period and re-sells for 150,000 pesos.

What effect would a devaluation of the peso of 30% have on each business?

_____

_____

_____

The answer can be found on page 121.

Overall, you will probably have concluded that Mr Wilson was notionally correct so far as the market trader is concerned. Because he buys and sells locally and deals only in the local currency, the devaluation has no direct effect on this business.

But what happens if he has to buy imported diesel fuel for his vehicles, or a new van imported from Japan or Germany?

The peso in his pocket will then buy a lot less than it did before, even if his overseas supplier is willing to accept a currency in which confidence has been lost.

5.4 The World Trade Organization (WTO)

In 1995, the World Trade Organization (WTO) succeeded the General Agreement on Tariffs and Trade (GATT), which had similar aims and objectives.

The aim of the WTO is to promote trade among all the world's nations, free of artificial tariff barriers erected to protect local businesses in some countries. Based in Geneva, its remit covers services, physical goods and intellectual property.

Its role is a sensitive one, for it is often required to arbitrate between the competing interests of individual countries or the richer nations as a group and the poorer ones which depend on them as export markets for commodities such as rubber, coffee (of which the USA, for example, is a nett importer), bananas, rice, cocoa and metal ores.

The WTO faces dilemmas in:

- agriculture;
- textiles;
- clothing.

It could have a significant effect on your organization's business if it is involved in any way, directly or indirectly, in these business sectors.

The USA argues strongly in favour of unfettered world trade. However, in 2002, it imposed tariffs on imported steel and increased subsidies to its farmers. It also gave massive support to US airlines in the aftermath of the 11th September 2001 terrorist attacks. Free trade is a doctrine that many nations find much easier to preach than to practise.

Perhaps the real problem is that everyone agrees that free trade is a good thing until it affects their direct interests.

Countless bottles of wine are produced throughout the world every year by the *methode champenoise*, using the classic champagne grapes, Pinot Noir and Chardonnay, yet only those bottles produced in a small and rigidly defined area of northern France are allowed to be called 'champagne'.

Blue cheese is produced in many areas of the world, but only that made in the English county of Rutland and a small part of Leicestershire may be called 'Stilton'.

'Basmati' as a name can only be applied to long grain rice from a particular region of the Indian sub-continent. Rice imported into the UK is tested to ensure that it is genuine and thus merits the name and the premium price charged.

Bananas grown in former British and French Caribbean colonies, for example, the Windward Islands, have been given privileged access to European markets. American companies which run huge plantations on the mainland of South America wish to change those arrangements on the grounds that they restrict free trade.

The producers of all these items and many others have protected their brands on supposed quality grounds, securing employment for enormous numbers of people in their regions. But, for example, American agriculturists claim that rice which is technically identical to Basmati rice could be grown elsewhere in the world – possibly including the Southern USA. So why should the growers in Kashmir be allowed to restrain free trade by preventing others using the premium name?

This is the sort of problem which affects world trade every day of every year. You might think that, if Basmati rice could be produced elsewhere, making it cheaper to buy, that would be a good thing for any of a number of reasons. But would you be so broad minded if you worked in Melton Mowbray and found your market flooded with Anywheresville Stilton (as happens, for example, with Cheddar cheese) or in a Scotland awash with Pacific Basin 'Whisky' – especially if you work in the organizations affected? And what about the rice growers in Kashmir? They are much poorer than people in the Southern USA already. What would they do if their major cash crop diminished in demand, or its price fell dramatically?

Banana growers on mainland South America are not rich men, so why should they not be able to sell their produce on an equal footing with those from the Caribbean Islands? But the island growers are small farmers, without access to the capital provided by the corporations, and with nothing else to do if their main cash crop disappears.

These examples illustrate the complexity of world trade. In the WTO the most complex economic, political, moral, social and sheer survival issues have to be addressed on every working day. There are no right answers which can satisfy everyone.

5.5 The Organisation for Economic Co-operation and Development (OECD)

The OECD comprises 30 member countries which between them produce two-thirds of the world's goods and services (they are also, of course, involved with the WTO and the UN.) As the name suggests, the OECD is involved with channelling support to developing nations, many of whom have strong cultural and economic ties already to European states such as Spain, Portugal and France. It is much concerned with issues affecting international commerce, including biotechnology, sustainable development and food safety.

The OECD is often accused of being a rich man's club, but that is too simplistic a view. As the examples illustrating the problems faced by the WTO show, there are no simple answers to world economic problems, and there is a need for the wealthier nations to assist long-term development in poorer ones. There is now general acceptance by the richer countries that with great privilege and power goes at least **some** responsibility.

Activity 34

3 mins

What do the following sets of initials stand for?

IBRD _____

IMF _____

OECD _____

WTO _____

IDA _____

The answers are given on page 121.

5.6 Globalization and the multinational corporations

All the bodies so far described are run by, or on behalf of, countries. They are well known and many of their activities are fairly public. They are not profit making, in the sense that they have no shareholders to whom they owe a duty to optimize profits.

But in recent years many huge multinational corporations, largely privately owned, have developed which are very powerful and influential in world politics and economics.

When did Globalization begin?

Multinationals are not a new phenomenon. The example of the South Sea Company given in Session A was a genuine international trading company before it was inflated into the first great financial scandal. The eighteenth-century East India Company had an honourable record and was one of the mainsprings of the British Empire.

In later centuries, British and French engineers helped to build railways, canals, roads and other infrastructure projects throughout the world. When oil became the dominant source of energy, the companies which tapped this vast resource had to be internationally minded. Many of the countries which used oil had none of their own and had to operate overseas.

Shipping companies have always been global in character. This has led to benefits to marine safety standards that are generally recognized throughout the world, saving countless lives at sea. Similar safety benefits flowed from the globalization of air traffic control, at the instigation of public and private airlines.

These are many examples of the transfer of plants from their original habitats to countries whose land and climate were suitable and which had sufficient labour to cultivate them.

Early moves towards globalization brought many economic benefits to countries such as India and Sri Lanka (which produced cotton and tea), Guyana (cane sugar), Colombia (coffee), Malaysia (rubber) and Kenya (coffee and tea). The examples are so numerous that they would fill a book by themselves. The members of OPEC, the Organization of Petroleum Exporting Countries, including Saudi Arabia, have become rich and influential nations in a matter of generations. Oil wealth is now enabling states such as Dubai to look beyond the time when the oil runs out, as illustrated in an earlier case study.

The question of Genetically Modified (GM) foods, developed by American multinationals and grown throughout the USA was one of the burning issues in 2002. With GM food, say the Americans, we could feed the world. Maybe, say a vast number of the UN's 191 members – but at what cost to the environment, freedom of choice and long-term human health. At root, the suspicion is that private short-term profits rather than altruism are driving the corporations.

Why is it so contentious now?

How has so much changed to make the operations of modern multinationals a subject of so much debate and acrimony?

It is easier to pose the question than to answer it. Take one of the earlier examples – coffee. It was grown in limited quantities in middle eastern countries such as Yemen. It is possible that those countries would have prospered more by selling limited amounts of coffee as a premium product, had it not become a commodity grown in Brazil and other countries.

It is impossible to rewrite history, so there can be no answers to such questions. They have to be faced and are at the root of many political problems which plague the twenty-first century.

The UK itself has received large scale overseas investment from many countries. You may work for an organization from overseas yourself and so have personal experience to draw upon.

Perhaps the concept of the floating factory already referred to and the rapidity with which international corporations can move their activities now make them objects of suspicion. People don't forget that disasters such as the Exxon Valdez oil spillage in Alaska, the Bhopal chemical plant explosion in India and Thalidomide in the UK and other countries, all resulted from the failures of international corporations.

- Many call centres have been moved from UK sites to English-speaking countries, including India and Malaysia where graduate-level employees are recruited at a fraction of the cost of personnel in the UK. Staff are given orientation training about current issues and interests in the UK, including sports, pop music and the weather. Land prices are lower and much of the equipment is manufactured in the Far East – so all three factors of production are readily available at advantageous prices.
- An American cherry grower in a rocky, sparsely populated western state is finding his market shrinking as processors and supermarkets import fruit from the Far East. His land, though abundant, is unsuitable for other purposes, and a way of life that has existed for generations is threatened.
- Russia now exports armaments worth $2.5 billion per annum, including a large number of tanks. Many of these are built using prison labour, paid a fraction of the cost of labour in Europe or the USA. The workforce is skilled – and unlikely to go on strike.

These cases are chosen to show that globalization is a global phenomenon that effects everybody. In the case of the call centres, some commentators believe that they will shift again within ten years, so any prosperity which they bring to their present host countries, though welcome, will be short lived.

Is it all about cheap labour?

No labour is cheap if it cannot do the job to the right quality standards, so it isn't that simple, but standards are improving all the time. Car plants in South Korea and Taiwan work to the same stringent standards as European ones and are just as likely to have the equivalent of ISO 9000 quality systems.

As far as protecting the environment is concerned, an increasing number of Asian manufacturers work to the environmental standard equivalent of ISO 14001, so it may be unfair to accuse all Pacific rim companies of ravaging their environments and adding to the Asian cloud of pollution which featured in much media coverage in 2002.

Universal English – a two edged sword?

English has become virtually the universal language of commerce, a great boon and blessing to English and American business people who are unable or unwilling to learn other languages. But is there a downside for us in having a large percentage of the world's population speaking English?

Activity 35 · 3 mins

Can you suggest two or three possible economic **advantages** which the wide use of English may give to countries other than the UK and the USA? Think of speaking, reading and writing English.

_____

_____

_____

> Many Chinese children are now being taught English in anticipation of developing trade links with the USA, UK and all other nations where English is used.

You may have suggested that:

- the use of **spoken** English makes it relatively simple for people in many countries to take over jobs which involve only telephone contact with customers. These could involve call centres, customer care operations and financial services such as insurance. It can also encourage tourism in countries which increasingly make things easy for English speakers;
- being able to **read** English makes it simple to understand product specifications, contracts, technical manuals and reference books and therefore produce goods using high-tech Western machines;
- being able to **write** English means that business letters can be produced accurately and intelligibly to customers anywhere in the English-speaking world. English spell checkers built into computers make the process simpler.

The ease of communication which makes it simple for English speakers to communicate throughout the world can rebound on such countries as the USA and the UK since other countries, now including China, see the teaching of English as encouraging the floating factories and offices to land on their shores, and therefore benefiting their economies at the expense of the traditionally English-speaking nations.

5.7 International crime

While the multinational corporations provide legitimate employment, pay taxes and can be held legally accountable in the countries in which they operate, there is one increasingly influential aspect of international trade which cannot be ignored.

As the people who engage in international crime render no accounts, pay no taxes and recognize no laws, no statistics are available to show how much the trade amounts to. Nevertheless, every estimate made shows that hundreds or thousands of billions of pounds are involved each year.

The people who run international crime syndicates have also tried – and sometimes succeeded – in penetrating governments and influencing political and economic policy.

Activity 36 · 3 mins

Suggest what some of the main areas of international crime might be, and how they might affect the UK's economic activity. Indicate if your own organization suffers ill effects specifically from any of them.

_____

_____

_____

_____

International crime is involved in most or all of the activities which legitimate businesses deal with, so the list could be a long one. Some of the most lucrative and most threatening for organizations and governments are:

■ illegal drugs – now one of the world's largest international trades;
■ counterfeit goods – CDs, designer brands, computer software;
■ armaments – a vast trade, fuelled by the break-up of the former Soviet Union;
■ smuggling of items carrying high excise duties – tobacco, alcohol, fuel;
■ people – for purposes including illegal immigration, slave labour, vice;
■ piracy – which is increasing in frequency in various parts of the world;
■ kidnapping for ransom – endemic in some countries and a great deterrent to investment by legitimate businesses.

The effect on legitimate organizations and markets throughout the world can be enormous. For example:

- illegal drugs can reduce or destroy the effectiveness of employees, deter potential tourists from visiting known trouble spots, cause crime and increase taxes spent on preventive measures. Police time can be diverted, leading to increases in general crime, which increases costs generally;
- the colossal trade in counterfeit CDs, videos, smuggled goods and people can have serious financial effects on organizations, directly and indirectly. Counterfeit goods and designer labels can ruin local markets and threaten legitimate employment;
- smuggling again reduces the market for legitimate goods; reduces the collection of excise duties and leads to increases in general taxation
- illegal immigrants, who work in countries all over the world, have no employment rights and must work for whatever they are offered – destroying local jobs and standards of living;
- virtual slave labour drives down costs of commodities and makes it hard for legitimate businesses to compete.
- though organized crime syndicates pay no taxes, they understand the economic principles of supply and demand. For example, whole crops of drugs have been systematically destroyed to keep the price up and prevent the market becoming saturated – as was done with coffee stocks in Brazil in the 1930s for the same economic reason;
- many farmers in poor countries, from Afghanistan to Burma to Colombia, are caught between a rock and a hard place:
  - they can choose to grow legitimate crops, for which the price paid may hardly offer them a subsistence income, or
  - they can grow opium, marijuana or other crops for the drugs trade, earning much greater returns, but with the dual risk of having their crops destroyed entirely by the authorities and putting themselves in the hands of the criminals.

There is no doubt that key global issues now include:

- helping poor farmers out of the dilemma described by allowing them to earn a decent living from growing legitimate crops;
- curbing the demand for illegal drugs as well as punishing their suppliers;
- tackling the problem of high unemployment which encourages desperate people to seek **any** employment (whether legal or illegal) in the absence of the social security provisions taken for granted in Western countries;
- co-operating to prevent international crime, even where national interests might be served by turning a blind eye in the short term;
- educating people in the developed world to look hard at where the products which they consume come from.

The turnover of international crime is now so vast that it has to be considered as a key global issue alongside the economic and environmental issues which present major challenges for the twenty-first century.

6 The trade cycle, unemployment and economic growth

6.1 The trade cycle

Economists define the trade cycle as a period of prosperity, followed by a period of depression, separated by transitional periods of downturn and upturn.

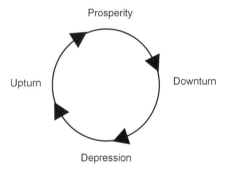

In principle, the idea is hardly new – the Biblical seven lean years following seven fat years is thousands of years old, but very similar in concept.

The trade cycle is much easier to theorise about than to measure. It is like high or low morale, which is easy to recognize when you see it but difficult to quantify.

Certainly, the Great Depression of 1929–1933 was easy enough to recognize, with massive unemployment, bank and business failures, and tangible poverty on the streets of countries in several continents. It followed the boom of 1925–1929, when it had seemed impossible for share prices ever to fall again and you simply had to keep on buying.

If the trade cycle really lasts for ten years, as some economists have argued, then the world has gone through seven cycles between 1932 and 2002. They were punctuated by the upheavals of World War Two (1939–1945) and many other smaller wars, in Korea, Vietnam, Iran/Iraq, the Balkans, Falkland Islands, the Middle East and many countries in Africa.

All of these wars have distorted the picture and make it impossible to draw a neat picture showing the peaks and troughs of the last 70 years

J.K. Galbraith, the American economist who lived through the Great Depression and saw the Internet bubble burst 70 years later, said: 'Show me an economic genius and I'll show you a rising market'.

A common factor does seem to be that, during boom years, unrealistic expectations are raised. Share prices increase, people sell them to other people who buy at a higher price in the expectation that prices will rise yet more, and so they do – until confidence, the key word in all economics, evaporates like a morning mist in August – and bust follows.

Meanwhile, underlying trading profits, those essential lubricants of economic activity which many of you work to help produce, decline and are ignored until it is clear that no one is making a return on their investment. Share price inflation can then be seen for what it is – a bubble of gas fuelled by the oxygen of get-rich-quick investors, encouraged by foolhardy advisors – or worse, advisors driven by the prospect of lucrative commissions.

> The South Sea Bubble, the Great Depression and the aftermath of the Internet boom – which in some ways raised the most unrealistic expectations of all – shared similar characteristics of share price increases which had nothing to do with operating profits. At the height of the Internet boom company proprietors were arguing that not only did profits not matter, neither did sales. All was based on their predictions of obtaining, at some time in the future, a huge share of a supposedly infinite market.
>
> Eventually, with no prospect for many of them ever making a profit, investors lost confidence, panicked and fell over each other to offload the shares for whatever they would fetch. The bubble, once again, had burst.

In the real world, politicians, business and trades union leaders in many countries have laboured long and with some success to mitigate the effects of the trade cycle. In particular, they have tried to lessen the distance between the peaks and troughs and make the slopes of the upturns and downturns less steep.

6.2 Unemployment

EXTENSION 6
This extension provides comparative figures for unemployment in the UK, some EU countries, the USA and other countries referred to in this workbook.

Rising unemployment is a classic sign of economic downturn. High unemployment is associated with depression, and its opposite with prosperity.

But what is 'high' and what is 'low' and how do you measure unemployment? Of course, we are back to Disraeli's dictum about 'lies, damned lies and statistics'. Politicians of all parties try to make the figures prove what they want them to prove. Nevertheless, over a period, the trends tend to emerge with reasonable credibility.

Activity 37

5 mins

Using the information from Extension 6 (page 114), please say:

1 Which EU country has the highest unemployment figure?

_____

2 Which of the following countries has the lowest unemployment figure.

Italy   South Africa   Switzerland   France   Japan

3 What is the average unemployment figure for EU members?

_____

4 By how many percentage points does the UK's unemployment figure vary from the European norm?

+3.4   +5.4   –5.4   –2.4   –3.4   +2.4

5 Which of the following countries has the highest unemployment figure:

Argentina   Italy   Norway   Poland   South Africa   USA.

The answers are given on page 122.

Unemployment is a scourge in many countries, and figures like those which you have seen for Argentina, Poland, Spain and South Africa would be completely unacceptable here. It is important to distinguish between short-term and long-term unemployment, however.

In any economy, no matter how healthy it may be, there will be a level of unemployment.

Inevitably, some companies close or contract in size. Some people simply decide to change their job or move to another part of the country and take a while to find a job there. There can be any number of reasons for unemployment.

Real problems arise when there is high long-term employment which becomes a fact of economic life (often called **structural unemployment**). It may happen in relation to a particular area of a country or, worse still, to the whole of a country, with the risk of political turmoil.

6.3 Economic growth

Promoting economic growth has been one of the primary aims of successive UK Governments in conjunction with policies aimed at controlling inflation and avoiding structural unemployment.

Most people would agree that growth is a desirable objective. Children, young animals, plants and trees are all expected to grow as a part of the natural order of things, so it is natural to think in such terms. In all these cases it is obvious that growth is taking place, but how do you encourage the economy to grow, and how do you recognize economic growth – or the reverse – when you see it ?

Encouraging growth

If you think back to the factors of production, you will realize that growth is about:

- stimulating investment in capital;
- making labour more productive.

So it is generally agreed that to promote growth, a government needs to:

- encourage nett savings (which are then invested in productive activities);
- encourage increased productivity among the workforce.

The third factor of production, land, is effectively a fixed resource unless you can reclaim it from the sea or acquire someone else's, as, for example, the USA did in the past by buying both Florida (from Spain) and Alaska (from Russia).

If you think for a moment about the two stimulants to growth (savings and productivity), it is obvious that they will not always be compatible with other economic objectives.

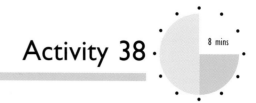

Activity 38

8 mins

Imagine that productivity in an engineering company making buses and coaches improves by 10% as a result of investment in more automated production lines. The company can now make 110 buses in the same time it formerly took to make 100.

What effect might this have on:

1 unemployment, assuming that the market for buses cannot be expanded and unemployment is running at around 8% nationally?

_____

_____

2 inflation, assuming that the employees' pay is increased by 8% and the market for buses can be expanded to take all the extra production? Assume that inflation, as normally reported, is running at 2.4%.

_____

_____

You most probably concluded that:

1 it is likely that some people will lose their jobs. They may take some time to find suitable alternative employment with unemployment already 3% higher than the current UK figure (2002);

2 as people are receiving pay rises well above the rate of inflation, they will have extra spending power – which may lead to demand pull inflation.

Of course, if either event were happening in just one factory, the effects on the UK's vast economy would be tiny. But if they applied to a significant sector of the economy, or in labour-intensive sectors such as teaching, medicine, public services or local/central government, they could have a significant effect on the economy as a whole. For example, replacing large numbers of teachers with technology-based teaching could create significant unemployment; awarding above-inflation pay rises to specific groups of workers could contribute to rising inflation levels when they begin to spend their increased pay.

Again, if people receiving the pay rises chose to spend a high proportion of the rise on overseas travel, or buy second homes in Florida or Spain, that would have an adverse effect on the balance of payments, which in turn could threaten the value of sterling and increase the price of essential imports such as food. As Table (b) in Extension 3 shows, the UK already has a food trade deficit of more than £8,000,000,000 per year. A 5% fall in the value of sterling could add a staggering £400,000,000 to that vast bill.

Economic contraction

The USSR example

The opposite of growth, contraction, can be very painful. It can be seen in the run-down economies of Russia and its former satellites – for example, Romania, Poland and East Germany. Capital resources used to be worked to exhaustion. Land was often badly farmed following the forced take over of private farms by gigantic collectives in the 1930s (which contributed to famine in the Ukraine, formerly the bread basket of Russia and possessing some of the most fertile land in Europe).

The productivity of labour was correspondingly low, and the lack of efficiency was matched by low wages. The potential structural unemployment was masked by the fact that all orders came from the central state who could tell factories to make steel or tractors or grow crops with no regard to the demand for them.

The raising of the iron curtain revealed a stage whose props comprise rusting, unsafe (or downright dangerous), environmentally disastrous, inefficient plant and factories plus a cast of demoralized workers whose productivity by world standards is so low that they cannot justify even the low wages they earn by comparison with the western world.

The evidence of mismanagement of the world's centralized command economies is there for all to see and contrasts with the prosperity enjoyed by the majority of Western Europeans.

6.4 Conclusion

This workbook has given many illustrations of the evils which mismanagement of the economy can create, whether in South America, Soviet Russia or the USA in the 1930s.

By and large, the UK has avoided the worst excesses of economic mismanagement and has one of the most stable systems of government in the world. Whether it continues to do so depends on its citizens. In a democratic system, governments ultimately are elected by the voters and can govern only with their consent.

Governments of every political party face the same problems of reconciling often unrealiztic desires with the practical needs of prudent government – and their desire to be re-elected.

The organization you work for is a part of the vast UK economy which has managed through two World Wars, many other conflicts, the transition from being an imperial power to the centre of a Commonwealth and a member of the EU.

The table below contrasts some of the competing desires of the electorate with the competing needs for good government.

Desires of electorate	**Needs of government**
Ever improving standards of material prosperity	Keep inflation under control and maintain international competitiveness
Lower taxes	Maintain public services and national defence
Full employment, or something approaching it	Prevent wage driven inflation and maintain mobility of labour
Spend your money as you wish	Protect the value of the £ sterling
Ever increasing expectations of health service, education and social services	Keep taxes to a level which the electorate will tolerate

John Stuart Mill, the nineteenth-century economist and writer said in his *Essay on Liberty*: 'The worth of a state, in the long run, is the worth of the individuals composing it'.

It seems an appropriate thought with which to end this workbook.

Self-assessment 2

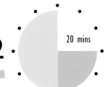

20 mins

1 Underline from the following list **three** examples of items which would increase the UK's imports, assuming that all the purchasers are UK residents:

- buying a meal in a restaurant in Brussels
- paying a train fare to travel from London to Edinburgh
- buying a bottle of German wine in a local supermarket
- sending flowers via the Internet to a relative who lives in Malaysia
- travelling to Florida on a British Airways flight.

2 The balance of _____ measures the overall difference between the UK's _____ and _____, including _____ or 'intangible' items.

3 More than 100 years ago the British Prime Minister, Benjamin _____ said that there are _____, _____ lies and _____.

4 Increases in the exchange rate of sterling against other currencies makes _____ goods and the cost of _____ travel _____ expensive.

5 Decreases in the exchange rate of sterling against other currencies makes _____ goods more _____ and _____ the costs of items such as overseas _____ rooms and fares on foreign _____.

6 The original impetus to establish the European Coal and Steel Community, the forerunner of the EU, was _____ _____.

7 The EU has endeavoured to provide _____ of movement for _____ and goods, a single _____ and political _____ for its member states.

8 _____ who sit in the _____ Parliament are the only people elected to any of the EU's key _____.

9 Give four examples of multinational corporations, including ones which affect your own organization directly or indirectly.

_____

_____

_____

_____

10 What are the four stages of the trade cycle?

_____

_____

_____

_____

11 The scale of international _____ is now so extensive that it can even affect the vast _____ of the most developed countries.

12 Underline the correct answer:

Structural unemployment occurs when:

■ people decide to change jobs or move to another part of the country;
■ people in large numbers cannot get jobs for many months or years;
■ some companies close or contract in size.

13 Symptoms of economic contraction include full order books, high levels of savings and investment, and low unemployment.

Do you agree with this statement ? Give your reasons.

_____

_____

_____

14 A common factor in boom years such as those of 1925 to 1929 seems to be the raising of _____ expectations and rises in _____ prices which bear no relation to _____ performance.

15 The near universal use of the _____ language makes it relatively simple to move _____ of many kinds from developed to _____ developed countries.

7 Summary

- The UK's prosperity depends on its continuing ability to trade successfully with the rest of the world in its entirety.

- No one owes us a living, and increasing expenditure on health, education and social provisions generally must be paid for in the long term by economic activity.

- The continuing deficits on visible trade and balance of payments are a concern and could eventually put real pressure on the value of the pound sterling.

- The European Union (EU) began life in 1952 in the desire to end a century of warfare in Europe, especially involving economic disputes between France and Germany. By 2002, there had been 50 years of relative peace since the EU's inception.

- Further EU expansion from the 2002 membership of 15 countries is underway.

- The UK is a member of international organizations which contribute to and distribute aid to poorer countries.

- Globalization is not really a new phenomenon, but the motives of international corporations appear to be distrusted widely, despite the measurable economic contribution which they make to many countries, including the UK.

- International crime now operates on such a vast scale that it can influence the economic affairs of even the largest economies.

- The boom to bust characteristics of previous trade cycles were always associated with unrealiztic expectations of ever-rising share prices unrelated to real profits.

- Economic growth needs to be managed to avoid it leading to increasing inflation, unemployment and pressure on exchange rates.

- Countries such as Brazil and Argentina show just how badly and quickly things can go wrong when confidence in a currency is lost.

- The graphic examples of economic contraction in former USSR states show starkly the perils of centralized control which ignores what the market actually demands of an economy.

- Governments of all parties in the UK are constantly trying to reconcile ever-increasing demand for public services with the electorate's unwillingness to pay for them.

- The UK's long-term prosperity depends on political stability and the ingenuity, efficiency and good sense of its people.

Performance checks

1 Quick quiz

Question 1   Economics is often called the 'gloomy science' because it _____ people to confront _____ which they hope will go way. But they _____.

Question 2   Allocate the following items to one of the three factors of production.

- garage forecourt
- sheep pasture
- garage mechanic
- airline pilot

- delivery vehicle
- computer programmer
- industrial robot
- bulldozer

- power station
- development site
- stagehand
- airfield

Land	Labour	Capital

Question 3   Land in the UK is some of the most _____ land in the world because of the UK's _____ population _____.

Question 4   Give three examples of the way in which labour may be rewarded, other than through wages and salary payments.

_____

_____

_____

Question 5   What do you understand by the term 'floating factory'?

_____

_____

Question 6   Under a state directed or 'command' economy, the state acquires the means of _____, _____ and _____, and makes virtually every economic decision _____.

Question 7   In a mixed or free 'market' economy, the _____ mechanism keeps _____ and _____ in balance.

Question 8   The government's published _____ figures are generalized, reflecting the overall economy. In reality, each _____ and _____ has its own _____ figure.

Question 9   Why is it essential for countries to achieve stable economic conditions over extended periods of time?

_____

_____

_____

_____

Question 10   The loss of confidence in a country's _____, the management of its economy or the _____ of its business leaders can quickly destroy its prosperity and create political and civil unrest.

Question 11   The balance of _____ trade shows the monetary difference between what the UK _____ and _____ in visible/physical or 'tangible' goods.

Question 12   In the following list underline three items which would reduce the UK's balance of payments deficit.

- relocating a call centre formerly operated in Aberdeen to New Delhi
- charging interest on a loan made by a UK bank to a Dutch shipping company
- increasing the number of American visitors to the UK by 5%
- replacing English coal-fired power stations with more efficient ones fuelled with gas from Norwegian oil and gas fields
- increasing the number of UK citizens who take holidays in Scotland, rather than going to other European countries
- equipping the new House of Commons members' facilities with furniture made from Brazilian hardwoods

Question 13   From Extension 3 Table (b) state for 2000:

a which was the UK's largest category of exports?

_____

b in which category did the UK have the largest surplus?

_____

c which category produced the largest trade deficit?

_____

d what was the surplus or deficit on food, drink and tobacco?

_____

Question 14   _____ is not a new phenomenon, and many _____ countries have benefited from the activities of organizations which operate globally.

Question 15   What two things must a government do to promote economic growth? What may be the consequences of growth which is too rapid?

_____

_____   _____

_____

_____

_____

Answers to these questions can be found on pages 122–23.

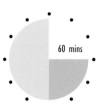

60 mins

2 Workbook assessment

Read the following case study and then deal with the questions which follow, writing your answers on a separate sheet of paper.

Mike Carlisle and Shidu Razan left the electrical engineering company in North London for which they worked to set up their own business, Enlightened Enterprises, manufacturing table lamps in a rented industrial unit. Shidu had contacts in the Middle East and they soon began to export a proportion of their output in addition to selling to local hardware and lighting shops with whom they had prudently established contact before setting out on their own. Mike's sister, Frances, sorted out the complex export documentation for them and looked after the UK sales. They manufactured to recognized British Standards and instituted a quality system of their own based on ISO 9000 procedures, though they did not go to a formal, externally assessed system. The business grew steadily in the first few months.

After about a year they were approached by a multiple retailer who had become aware of their products and thought them very good. They were offered a substantial contract to supply lamps via a distribution warehouse in Rugby. About half the lamps were going to European stores. Though they had to spend money on equipment and larger premises, and recruit and train new staff, they decided it was an excellent opportunity. The lamps were supplied subject to three months' written notice on either side.

All went well for three years and the multiple business reached 80% of their total sales. Their own export business stayed much the same after the first year, mainly because they had no time to pursue it while meeting the demands of their major customer.

At the beginning of March, a letter arrived from their major customer saying that they had found an alternative source of lamps at substantially lower cost. Their stores in Europe were to close, as had been announced in the press. By the terms of the contract, this letter was to give them three months' formal notice. Purchases would be scaled down in anticipation of the European closure which reflected the high price of sterling purchases.

Shidu and Mike found themselves staring disaster in the face. They had invested heavily, and now employed 16 staff on UK-level salaries and employment terms. They were to lose 40% of their business immediately and a further 40% in three months' time. A phone call to one of their immediate contacts revealed that the new suppliers were in China and the Philippines.

The facts reflect the dilemma faced by many UK businesses, large and small and are based on a real situation.

In the light of what you have been studying in this workbook, analyse the situations which the partners have faced at three points in the life cycle of their business:

- when they agreed to take on the extra business;
- as they expanded it to become the dominant part of their business;
- when faced with the loss of 80% of their business.

1 Look at each of these situations together with the factors of production involved, i.e. land, capital and labour, and suggest what, if anything, they might have done differently to achieve a happier outcome.

2 What legal and international factors have influenced their situation?

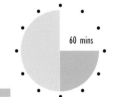

60 mins

3 Work-based assignment

The time guide for this assignment reflects how long it may take you to write up your findings. You will need to spend additional time gathering information, talking to colleagues and thinking through the data you have assembled. Some of the information may be regarded as confidential, though much will be available from published annual accounts and employee reports or company newsletters in publicly run organizations.

If some information is unobtainable for reasons of confidentiality, then you should indicate this in your answer.

If the categories given miss some aspects of what your organization does, write down the information for these on a separate sheet

Your written response to this assignment may form useful evidence for your S/NVQ portfolio. The assignment is designed to help you demonstrate the following Personal Competences:

- searching for information;
- thinking and taking decisions.

What you should do

This workbook has shown that all organizations are affected by the economic environment in which they operate. The economic environment now includes the entire world which has become a 'global village'. It has also shown that all organizations use the three factors of production in some combination with raw materials which vary according to their activities.

You are now asked to look at your own organization and the impact which external factors have had, using the chart provided on the facing page to summarize your conclusions.

If you conclude that there has been no effect in some cases, please say so and be prepared to back up your statement

Economic influence:	Effect on your organization over the past 2 or 3 years		
	None	Some	Details (or reasons why none)
Fiscal Policy: ■ Direct, e.g. Corporation Tax/ Employer's NI ■ Indirect, e.g. VAT			
Monetary policy: Interest rate movements			
Inflation			
Exchange rate movements			
Competition: ■ from the UK ■ from the EU ■ from elsewhere			
UK and European Law: ■ affecting people ■ affecting the environment ■ affecting the way the organization is run			
Common Agricultural Policy (CAP)			
Globalization: ■ Inward investment ■ Transfer of facilities abroad			

Reflect and review

1 Reflect and review

This workbook began with a quote from an interview given by Sir Alec Douglas Home. The same Prime Minister said during a speech in his constituency:

'There are two problems in my life. The political ones are insoluble and the economic ones are incomprehensible'.

This book might have confirmed his view of the political problem, but hopefully might have helped him to comprehend at least some of the economic concepts.

Now that you have completed your work on organizational environment let's review the workbook objectives.

The first objective was:

■ list the fundamental factors of production and be able to relate them to your own organization and everyday working life

Every organization uses the three factors of production: land, capital and labour in conjunction with raw materials in order to produce its goods and services.

■ Do you now have a clear understanding of the basic factors of production? Is it clear that they are used by every organization in some combination to produce goods and services?

_____

_____

_____

The second objective was:

■ outline the eternal economic problems and the limited range of political measures available to tackle them.

The UK economy is so vast and so complex that it is impossible to plan and regulate in detail. The command economies of the Soviet Union and communist China have learned by bitter experience that central planning is difficult or impossible to make work, even in a totalitarian state of the kind which we have never permitted to arise.

Governments have a limited range of levers available, which you have had chance to examine, including fiscal (or taxation) polices to control disposable incomes, monetary policy which influences interest and exchange rates, and laws regulating the activities of utility providers and organizations generally, to protect the general public both from the companies' activities and their own gullibility and greed. It was stressed that government has no money of its own and can only spend in the long term what individual electors are prepared to tolerate through the taxes they pay.

You might like to think about:

The third objective was:

■ recognize the important economic and political factors which affect your organization

This book should have both confirmed and expanded your knowledge of the way in which political and economic events in this country and overseas influence the work of your organization, whatever business it is involved in.

Things to think about include:

■ How do you now intend to expand your knowledge further and keep abreast of significant changes which affect you and the organization for which you work?

_____

_____

_____

The fourth workbook objective was:

■ explain the effect of currency exchange rates on organizations in all countries

A reduction in the value of a currency always has serious consequences for a country, making essential imports expensive and undermining confidence in the local economy. The collapse of a currency, such as happened in Germany after World War One, can cause misery and desperation on such a scale that governments are destabilized. There is then a risk of a demagogue such as Hitler or Mussolini rising to power, with unpredictable and potentially catastrophic consequences.

The UK has never experienced a collapse in the value of sterling, though there have been devaluations, and the pound has depreciated over many years against the US dollar.

Consider the following question:

■ How will you now try to monitor the effects of fluctuations in exchange rates on your organization and its situation in the economy?

_____

_____

_____

The next objective was:

■ describe the structure of the EU and its impact on the UK and its business

The EU was born out of the desire by statesmen from six war-ravaged European countries to make war in Europe inconceivable. It began life as the European Coal and Steel Community in 1952. The UK joined in 1973, following a referendum. The EU has a mix of economic, administrative and political aims which often conflict with the wishes of individual member states. Collectively, the EU is now the UK's largest trading partner and decisions taken here on legal, political and economic issues are increasingly determined – or strongly influenced by – policies agreed by the Council of Ministers.

Ask yourself the following questions:

■ Do you understand the structure and operations of the EU clearly and the impact which it has had in changing the UK's way of running its affairs? Is it clear what affect the EU has on your own organization's operations? How will you maintain a continuing interest to enable you to enter into an informed debate over issues such as the potential entry of the UK into the Eurozone and the proposed continuing expansion of EU membership?

_____

_____

_____

The next objective was:

■ identify the influences beyond the EU which are significant for UK business

The UK trades with virtually every country in the world and has strong ties with more than 50 Commonwealth countries and the USA, its largest individual trading partner. In consequence, nothing significant happens anywhere in the world which could not have an effect on our economy – from natural disasters to political upheavals to the erection of trade barriers and the activities of international criminals.

Things to think about include:

■ Do you have a clearer understanding of the global issues facing your own organization and UK businesses and general standards of living?

_____

_____

_____

Have you developed some ideas which could help to meet the challenges? How will you be taking a continuing interest in matters which affect everyone in the UK, but are often ignored by the mass media?

_____

_____

_____

The last objective was:

■ outline the effect which the globalization of business has on local organizations throughout the world.

Organizations which operate globally are often much larger than the economies of developing countries and have no electorate to answer to. Many such companies operate in the UK and some global companies are also based here. Too many of the comments made about them are in the form of simplistic slogans, and many multinationals have achieved much that is good in developed and developing countries, But they have been associated with disasters such as Bhopal and Thalidomide, and are increasingly able to move their operations around the world using the floating factory concept. They are frequently objects of suspicion and pilloried by environmental and other pressure groups.

Ask yourself the following question:

■ Do you now have a better understanding of the scope and potential impact of such organizations generally, and as they affect your own organization's activities?

_____

_____

_____

2 Action plan

Use this plan to further develop for yourself a course of action you want to take. Make a note in the left-hand column of the issues or problems you want to tackle, and then decide what you want to do, and make a note in column 2.

The resources you need might include time, materials, information or money. You may need to negotiate for some of them, but others could be easy to acquire, like half an hour of somebody's time, or a chapter of a book. Put whatever you need in column 3. No plan means anything without a timescale, so put a realistic target completion date in column 4.

Desired outcomes			
1 Issues	2 Action	3 Resources	4 Target completion
Actual outcomes			

3 Extensions

Extension 1

Some UK regulatory bodies and legal measures used by the UK Government

Companies Acts 1948 – 1998
A succession of Acts has regulated the way in which companies behave, and amendments are made as practices formerly acceptable become less so, or governments discover other ways in which the letter and spirit of earlier legislation is being flouted.

In particular, the Acts regulate:

- the issue of prospectuses inviting the public to subscribe for shares;
- what a company can and cannot do under its certificate of incorporation;
- how the authority to manage its affairs is to be divided between the shareholders and directors;
- directors' powers to raise capital.

It is very necessary to have close regulation of limited liability companies. They are treated as having an identity in law separate from their owners and managers, unlike a sole trader or members of a partnership. This continues to cause difficulty, for example, in knowing whom (if anyone) to prosecute for manslaughter following disasters such as rail crashes where lives are lost and where the business is operated by a limited liability company.

Competition Act 1998
This is new law, akin to that which is used in Europe to check organizations exploiting a dominant monopolistic position enjoyed by a number of co–operating suppliers, for example, in professions such as architecture and accountancy. The law is enforced by the Director General of Fair Trading, and a new Competition Commission has been established to succeed the Monopolies and Mergers Commission.

Restrictive Trade Practices Acts 1956–1976
This legislation outlaws practices concerned with price fixing between ostensibly competing suppliers. The law is enforced by the Restrictive

Practices Court. Suppliers have in the past tried both to maintain prices at levels higher than competition would allow and to prevent retailers selling products below the price they have set, for example, by collectively withdrawing supplies. The 1976 Act extends the scope of the legislation to include service agreements.

Resale Prices Act 1964

This Act forbids manufacturers to set minimum recommended prices for their goods or to enforce such prices through sanctions such as lower discounts to sellers who ignore the recommended price levels. There are exemptions in the case of books which still apply in 2002. Currently, there are often recommended retail prices, which are in effect **maximum** prices, rather than the **minimum** prices set by organizations before the abolition of resale price maintenance.

Fair Trading Act 1973

This Act established the office of Director General of Fair Trading to adjudicate in cases of monopoly. Monopoly is more stringently defined as being a 25% share of the market (formerly 33%). Proposed mergers which have monopolistic implications can be referred to the Director General for adjudication. The existence of this legislation acts as a deterrent to companies that may have less than honourable reasons for wishing to merge.

Competition Commission (formerly the Monopolies and Mergers Commission)

As its name implies, the Competition Commission is charged with looking into a wide range of practices which restrict competition and to decide whether any public interest is served by such practices. Company directors can be ingenious at finding ways of co-operating to flout the spirit of the law, even if they are seemingly obeying its letter. This makes the Commission's task very hard. The welter of information involved in large company operations and the spin which can be put on the facts to support a case on whose success may depend billions of pounds can make it virtually impossible to see the true position.

Financial Services Authority (FSA)

The FSA was established in 1997 and is charged with overseeing the activities of the financial sector, including banking, insurance, pensions, building societies and companies trading in securities. The FSA has not been viewed as an unqualified success but, given the complexities of intangible financial products such as endowment policies and unit trusts, it is hardly surprising that it is difficult for **any** body to keep watch over such a complex field.

Extension 2

Title: *Annual abstract of statistics*
Publisher: The Stationery Office
Edition: 2002

Extension 3   Some UK trading figures

Table (a) Imports and exports – total figures
(all figures given in £ billions)

Balance of visible trade	1997	1998	1999	2000	2001
Goods exported (a)	172	164	166	188	191
Goods imported (b)	184	185	193	218	224
Surplus/(deficit) (c) = (a) + (b)	(12)	(21)	(27)	(30)	(33)
Cumulative deficit	(12)	(33)	(60)	(90)	(123)
Invisible items surplus/(deficit) **(d)**	10	16	8	13	13
Balance of payments surplus/(deficit) (e) = (c) – (d)	(2)	(5)	(19)	(17)	(20)
Cumulative deficit	(2)	(7)	(26)	(43)	(63)

Table (b) Visible trade by type (2000)

Category	Imports (a)		Exports (b)		Surplus/(deficit) (a) – (b) £ billion
	£ billion	**% of total**	**£ billion**	**% of total**	
Machinery/vehicles	99.2	46	87.6	47	(11.6)
Manufactured goods	32.8	15	21.2	11	(11.6)
Manufactured materials	29.3	13	22.7	12	(6.6)
Chemicals, oils, fats	21.0	9	25.1	14	4.1
Food, drink, tobacco	18.0	8	9.9	5	(8.1)
Fuels	9.9	5	17.1	9	7.2
Raw materials	5.8	3	2.4	1	(3.4)
Miscellaneous	1.8	1	1.7	1	(0.1)
Totals	217.8	100	187.9	100	(30.0)

Table (c) UK imports and exports (2000)

£ billion – in descending order of UK exports

Country	Exports	Imports	Surplus/(deficit)
USA	29.4	28.5	0.9
Germany	22.7	27.7	(5.0)
France	18.5	18.2	0.3
Netherlands	15.1	15.1	0
Republic of Ireland	12.3	9.5	2.8
Belgium	10.3	11.6	(1.3)
Italy	8.4	9.4	(1.0)
Spain	8.3	6.0	2.3
Oil exporting countries	6.1	4.3	1.8
Sweden	4.2	4.9	(0.7)
Japan	3.7	10.2	(6.5)
Canada	3.5	4.0	(0.5)
Switzerland	3.1	5.5	(2.4)
Australia	2.7	1.5	1.2
Hong Kong	2.7	5.9	(3.2)
India	2.1	1.7	0.4
China	1.5	4.8	(3.3)
South Korea	1.4	3.4	(2.0)
Taiwan	1.0	3.6	(2.6)
Russia	0.7	1.5	(0.8)
Other countries	30.3	40.7	(10.4)
Totals	188	218	(30)

Extension 4

Some factors which give the USA economic advantage

Land:

- large land mass, relatively lightly populated;
- low costs of land in most areas for farming and industry;
- forms virtually an island, free of major threats on its borders with Canada and Mexico;
- few land borders; position encourages trade across both Pacific and Atlantic Oceans;
- varied climate, allowing growth of virtually any crop and every sort of holiday.

Labour:

- experienced, skilled workforce in many disciplines. Flexibility in working practices is common;
- has strong scientific base in all disciplines;
- expertise in production engineering and information technology;
- stable political system; commitment by large majority to a single cultural identity. Freedom from general war on its land mass since end of Civil War (1861–1865);
- until recently, English has been common language throughout entire population and the language of commerce almost everywhere.

Capital:

- vast industrial base developed over 100 years or more. Home to many multinational corporations;
- military and space research have driven technological development;
- highly developed communications infrastructure by every means;
- common currency throughout all states, enormous reserves of gold and foreign currency, no tariff barriers within whole vast economy;
- educational system developed over more than a century.

Resources:

- vast natural resources, including those in Alaska;
- food abundant, though some major imports – including coffee.

Extension 5   The European Union

Member states (2002)

Austria	Belgium	Denmark	Finland	France
Germany	Greece	The Netherlands	Ireland	Italy
Luxembourg	Portugal	Spain	Sweden	UK

The Treaty of Nice allows any European State with a proven democratic form of government to apply for membership and Turkey, which is chiefly in Asia, has also applied to join.

No country is allowed to join the EU unless it can prove to the existing members' satisfaction that it is a democracy.

Extension 6

Unemployment around the world (2001)
(as % of adult labour force – based on OECD figures. Members of the EU are italicized.)

Country	%	Country	%
Switzerland	2.6	*Eurozone average*	*8.5*
Norway	3.5	*France*	*9.0*
USA	4.8	*Italy*	*9.5*
Hong Kong	4.9	*Spain*	*13.1*
Japan	5.0	Poland	17.0
UK	5.1	Argentina	18.0
Sweden	*5.1*	South Africa	30.0 +
Germany	*7.9*		

4 Answers to self-assessment questions

**Self-assessment 1
on pages 44–6**

1 The three factors of production are:

- land;
- labour;
- capital.

2 Organizations may strive to become 'least cost producer' in their fields:

- to protect themselves against overseas competition;
- to retain business in the face of demands for lower prices from their customers.

3 a Examples of situations where land has been created include drainage of land in Holland and the English fen country, and the building of Hong Kong's airport in land reclaimed from the sea.

   b Examples of entrepreneurship which has discovered a profitable use for redundant or barren land include transformation of desert land in Dubai into leisure facilities, and conversion of derelict industrial sites in the UK into gardens, exhibition sites and sports facilities.

4   The factors of production differ from **RAW MATERIALS** in that the latter are **CONSUMED** in the process, whereas the former remain **AVAILABLE/READY** for further use.

5   Wheat, oil seed rape, tides and winds are all examples of **RENEWABLE** resources.

6   The non-renewable resources listed are natural gas, coal, crude oil and iron ore.

7   Other things being equal, the more **ABUNDANT/SCARCE** a factor of production becomes, the **LOWER/HIGHER** will be its **MARKET** price.

8   If the cost of labour becomes relatively **HIGH/EXPENSIVE**, organizations will seek to **REPLACE** it with **CAPITAL** equipment, or by finding people prepared to **WORK FOR LOWER RATES**.

9   Monopoly arises where a single supplier or co-operating group of suppliers control the production and/or distribution of goods or services and so can fix prices to suit themselves.

10   The genuine sets of initial relating to industry watchdogs are:

OFGEM – gas and electricity supply
OFTEL – telecommunications
OFWAT – water

11   Subsidies can distort the price mechanism and cause suppliers of goods or services to believe that their activities have a higher market price than they would really command. If and when the subsidy is removed, this can lead to a sharp fall in price and unpleasant consequences for the supplier. You may believe that state subsidies can be justified to help disadvantaged sectors of society, here or in other countries.

12   Examples of indirect competition could include:

■   for a bus operator in London, Manchester or Newcastle: taxis, tubes, trams;
■   for a fish and chip shop: any other fast food outlet, such as Indian or Chinese take-aways;
■   for a cinema: live theatre or home entertainments such as TV and home videos.

13   The levying of **DIRECT** taxes, such as income tax and **CORPORATION** tax are examples of the government's **FISCAL** policies in action.

14   Indirect taxes, such as **VAT** and **COUNCIL TAX/EXCISE DUTIES** are deemed to be **REGRESSIVE** because they bear more heavily on people with **LOWER** incomes.

15 Every government's dilemma concerning fiscal policy is that the electorate demand higher and higher levels of **PUBLIC SERVICES**, but are unwilling to see **TAXES** rise to pay for them.

16 The letters MPC stand for the Bank of England's **MONETARY POLICY COMMITTEE** which became independent of the government in 1997.

17 Exchange rates measure the relative **PURCHASING** power of two **CURRENCIES** and indicate the **UNDERLYING** strength of their economies.

18 Examples of cost push inflation might include rises in the prices material costs; rents; wage or salary rates; costs of replacing equipment, and increases in rates of VAT which have to be passed on to consumers.

Demand pull shows up clearly when anything is in short supply, as has happened with oil, housing and the prices paid by companies for licences to operate mobile phone systems.

Wage-related inflation has occurred in organizations which rely heavily on the labour factor of production, such as teaching, health provision and the services undertaken by local authorities.

19 Unemployment can arise from causes such as the **DEPLETION** of natural resources, the **REPLACEMENT/SUBSTITUTION** of labour with **CAPITAL** equipment, or the **RELOCATION** of activities elsewhere in pursuit of **CHEAPER** labour.

20 Uncontrolled or **HYPER** inflation inevitably leads to **MASS/HIGH** unemployment, which can **BRING DOWN/DESTABILIZE** governments and lead to **EXTREMIST REGIMES** gaining power.

Self–assessment 2 on pages 92–3

1 Three examples of items which would increase the UK's imports, assuming that all the purchasers are UK residents, are:

- buying a meal in a restaurant in Brussels;
- buying a bottle of German wine in a local supermarket;
- sending flowers via the Internet to a relative who lives in Malaysia.

2 The balance of **PAYMENTS** measures the overall difference between the UK's **IMPORTS** and **EXPORTS**, including **INVISIBLE** or 'intangible items'.

3 More than 100 years ago the British Prime Minister, Benjamin **DISRAELI** said that there are **LIES**, **DAMNED** lies and **STATISTICS**.

4 Increases in the exchange rate of sterling against other currencies makes **IMPORTED** goods and the cost of **FOREIGN/OVERSEAS** travel **LESS** expensive.

5　Decreases in the exchange rate of sterling against other currencies makes **IMPORTED** goods more **EXPENSIVE** and **INCREASES** the costs of items such as overseas **HOTEL** rooms and fares on foreign **AIRCRAFT/TRAINS**.

6　The original impetus to establish the European Coal and Steel Community, the forerunner of the EU, was **A HEARTFELT DESIRE TO REMOVE THE ECONOMIC CAUSE OF PERSISTENT WARS IN EUROPE –** or words to that effect.

7　The EU has endeavoured to provide **FREEDOM** of movement for **PEOPLE** and goods, a single **CURRENCY** and political **STABILITY** for its member states.

8　MEPs who sit in the **EUROPEAN** Parliament are the only people elected to any of the EU's key **INSTITUTIONS**.

9　The answer will vary according to who you work for, but might include Nestlé; Coca Cola; McDonalds; British American Tobacco (BAT), all large oil companies (BP; Texaco; Shell) Glaxo; Monsanto; car manufacturers such as Ford, Nissan, Toyota – as general examples of organizations operating in many countries and often several continents.

10　The normally agreed four stages of the trade cycle are:

- prosperity;
- downturn;
- depression;
- upturn.

11　The scale of international **CRIME** is now so extensive that it can even affect the vast **ECONOMIES** of the most developed countries.

12　Structural unemployment occurs when people in large numbers cannot get jobs for many months or years.

13　The statement is incorrect, as these would be symptoms of economic growth.

14　A common factor in boom years like those of 1925 to 1929 seems to be the raising of **UNREALISTIC** expectations and rises in **SHARE** prices which bear no relation to **UNDERLYING PROFIT** performance.

15　The near universal use of the **ENGLISH** language makes it relatively simple to move **JOBS** of many kinds from developed to **LESS** developed countries.

5 Answers to activities

Activity 3 on page 6

The answers are:

1 **L**and;
2 **C**apital;
3 **L**abour.

Activity 4 on page 7

Land	Capital	Labour
■ development site ■ agricultural field ■ garage forecourt ■ car park ■ riverside wharf	■ delivery vehicle ■ computer ■ combine harvester ■ power station ■ video camera	■ itinerant fruit picker ■ receptionist ■ shop worker ■ managing director ■ economist

Activity 7 on page 12

Organization	Land	Capital	Labour	Raw materials
Hospital	car park	X ray machine	surgeon	dressings
Call centre	office space	computerized switchboard	customer care assistant	standard letters
Internet marketing company	rented garage	computer	entrepreneur	goods delivery notes
Take-away pizza shop	rented shop	travelling oven	shop assistant	flour and water
Newspaper	print room	high speed press	sub editor	ink
Football club	football pitch	gymnasium	goalkeeper	practice balls

Activity 10 on page 18

The typical additional on costs which an employer may have to bear are:

1 employer's contribution to National Insurance Fund (NIC)
2 pension contribution
3 holiday pay
4 statutory sick pay
5 maternity leave cover
6 subsidised food/beverages.

Activity 12 on page 20

The most obvious answer is water. Following privatization, supply was taken over by local profit-making companies who effectively are the only suppliers in an extensive area. Unlike gas, electricity or railway travel, there is no substitute for water and no arrangements have been made for competing companies to use the same supply infrastructure – as happens with BT telephone lines.

The Government has recognized the possible consequences of this effective monopoly and appointed a regulator, OFWAT, to control prices and other aspects of their businesses. It has also removed the right of a supplier to cut off supply to a customer who does not pay – because of the essential nature of water and the public health implications of disconnection.

Activity 18 on page 33

The politician was Robert Walpole and he was speaking in 1720 of the Act which led to the notorious 'South Sea Bubble' which burst in 1721. Ironically, Walpole made money out of the speculation, the aftermath of which he dealt with after becoming effectively the first prime minister of Great Britain.

Activity 21 on page 38

Each unit of local currency is now worth 75/100 pence, or 75 pence. Therefore, to buy the same amount of goods from the UK, the other country must export 100/75, or 1.33 times as much. To sell one third more goods is an enormous task – and what happens if its potential buyer doesn't need or want them?

Activity 24 on page 51

Comparative answer

Imports		Exports	
Invisibles	**Visibles**	**Invisibles**	**Visibles**
Foreign holidays	Tropical fruits and vegetables	Tourism	Meat and meat products
Electricity	Cars and commercial vehicles	Banking services	Steel and construction materials
Shipping	Electrical goods – fridges, etc.	Insurance services	Chemical products – plastics,
Civil aviation	Oil and petrol	Airlines' earnings	Tobacco products
Financial services	Clothing and footwear	Shipping	Fuels

Activity 28 on pages 60–1

1 The country we have the largest trade deficit with is Japan, at £6.5 billion.

2 The country we have the largest trade surplus with is the Republic of Ireland, at £2.8 billion.

3 China, Hong Kong, South Korea and Taiwan together account for £11.1 billion of the total UK deficit.

4 As a percentage of the total UK deficit of £30 billion, these four countries account for 37%.

5 The countries with which the UK's trade is approximately in balance are the USA, France, Netherlands, Sweden, Canada, India and Russia. You may have included Italy, with whom we had a deficit of exactly £1 billion.

6 The UK's largest single trading partner is the USA, with £29.4 billion of exports and £28.5 billion of imports – a total trade flow of £57.9 billion.

Activity 29 on page 62

1 The UK's balance of visible trade with Sweden will tend to **worsen** because of the imports from Sweden.

2 Germany's balance of visible trade with Sweden will also tend to **worsen**.

3 UK Exports of visible trade items will **increase** somewhat, assuming that some of the company's 2000 suppliers are in the UK.

4 Sweden's balance of trade on visible items with China will tend to **worsen** given that many of the company's goods are imported from there.

5 The exchange rate of sterling against the Swedish Krona may depreciate **if** there are more imports of goods from Sweden than exports of goods manufactured here. In any event, the individual effect would be marginal.

Activity 30 on page 66

The rankings for UK trade with other EU States are as follows:

1	Republic of Ireland	surplus	£2.8 billion
2	Spain	surplus	£2.3 billion
3	France	surplus	£0.3 billion
4	Netherlands	in balance	
5	Sweden	deficit	(£0.7 billion)
6	Italy	deficit	(£1.0 billion)
7	Belgium	deficit	(£1.3 billion)
8	Germany	deficit	(£5.0 billion)

The EU Countries not listed are: Austria, Denmark, Finland, Greece, Luxembourg and Portugal.

Activity 31 on page 69

The answers for questions 1, 2 and 3 of this activity will vary according to where you live.

The answer to question 4 is (60,000,000/87) = 689,655 people represented by an MEP, compared with (60,000,000/659) – 91,047 for a Westminster MP.

The EU Members who have not so far had a President of the European Commission are: Austria, Denmark, Finland, Greece, Ireland, Portugal, Spain and Sweden.

Activity 32 on page 72

Three countries which have not applied for membership of the EU are:

- Norway – after a majority of its citizens voted to remain outside. Norway has abundant resources, including oil and natural gas, which are in demand throughout the world, and a very low population density – 4.5 million people in an area of 322,000 square kilometres.
- Switzerland – which is wary of any links which might undermine the jealously guarded neutrality, and its democratic process and financial stability.
- Iceland – which is not strictly a European state, sitting as it does in the North Atlantic between Europe and North America.

All three are prosperous countries which trade extensively with the EU, including the UK. In fact, Switzerland exports £5.5 billion's worth of tangible goods to the UK and in return imports £3.1 billion, our largest trade deficit with any European country other than Germany.

Activity 33 on page 76

1 The wine will be worth 30% less, and so to earn the same amount of sterling, the company will have to sell more than 7 million pesos' worth of wine – an enormous increase which is probably unachievable.

2 The fuel will cost around 28.5 million pesos – 8.5 million extra, which will probably have to be passed on to customers at the pumps, if they can afford to pay.

3 Because he both buys and sells in pesos, he would not be directly affected, other factors being equal.

Activity 34 on page 79

IBRD	= International Bank for Reconstruction and Development
IMF	= International Monetary Fund
OECD	= Organization for Economic Co-operation and Development
WTO	= World Trade Organization
IDA	= International Development Association

Activity 37 on page 87

1 Spain – 13.1%.

2 Switzerland – 2.6%.

3 8.5%.

4 The UK figure is lower than the average for the EU at –3.4% points.

5 South Africa, at 30% plus.

6 Answers to the quick quiz

Answer 1 Economics is often called the 'gloomy science' because it **FORCES** people to confront **ISSUES/FACTS** which they hope will go away. But they **WON'T**.

Answer 2

Land	Labour	Capital
■ garage forecourt ■ sheep pasture ■ development site ■ airfield	■ computer programmer ■ garage mechanic ■ stagehand ■ airline pilot	■ delivery vehicle ■ power station ■ industrial robot ■ bulldozer

Answer 3 Land in the UK is some of the most **EXPENSIVE** land in the world because of the UK's **HIGH** population **DENSITY**.

Answer 4 Other ways in which labour may be rewarded include royalties, commission, professional fees, piece work rates and bonuses.

Answer 5 A floating factory is a business that is able to 'sail' from one country to another, or one continent to another, in pursuit of the most profitable combination of land, capital and labour.

Answer 6 Under a state directed or 'command' economy, the state acquires the means of **PRODUCTION**, **DISTRIBUTION** and **EXCHANGE**, and makes virtually every economic decision **CENTRALLY**.

Answer 7   In a mixed or free 'market' economy, the **PRICE** mechanism keeps **DEMAND** and **SUPPLY** in balance.

Answer 8   The government's published **INFLATION** figures are generalized, reflecting the overall economy. In reality, each **INDIVIDUAL** and **ORGANISATION** has its own **UNIQUE** figure.

Answer 9   It is essential for countries to achieve stable economic conditions over extended periods of time so that conditions can be created where economic activity can thrive and governments can provide generally acceptable levels of service for health, education and other welfare provision.

Answer 10   The loss of confidence in a country's **CURRENCY**, the management of its economy or the **INTEGRITY** of its business leaders can quickly destroy its prosperity and create political and civil unrest.

Answer 11   The balance of **VISIBLE** trade shows the monetary difference between what the UK **IMPORTS** and **EXPORTS** in visible/physical or 'tangible' goods.

Answer 12   The three items which would reduce the UK's balance of payments deficit are:

- charging interest on a loan made by a UK bank to a Dutch shipping company;
- increasing the number of American visitors to the UK by 5%;
- increasing the number of UK citizens who take holidays in Scotland, rather than going to other European countries.

Answer 13   a The UK's largest category of exports was machinery and vehicles.
b The UK had its largest surplus in fuels.
c Two categories produced the equal largest trade deficit. They were machinery/vehicles and manufactured goods.
d The deficit on food, drink and tobacco was £8.1 billion.

Answer 14   **GLOBALISATION** is not a new phenomenon, and many **DEVELOPING** countries have benefited from the activities of organizations which operate globally.

Answer 15   The two things a government must do to promote economic growth are to:

- promote nett savings which flows into capital investment;
- increase the productivity of labour.

The undesirable consequences of growth which is too rapid could include:

- accelerating inflation;
- pressure on the sterling exchange rate.

7 Certificate

Completion of this certificate by an authorized person shows that you have worked through all the parts of this workbook and satisfactorily completed the assessments. The certificate provides a record of what you have done that may be used for exemptions or as evidence of prior learning against other nationally certificated qualifications.

Pergamon Flexible Learning and ILM are always keen to refine and improve their products. One of the key sources of information to help this process are people who have just used the product. If you have any information or views, good or bad, please pass these on.

INSTITUTE OF LEADERSHIP & MANAGEMENT

SUPERSERIES

Organizational Environment

....

has satisfactorily completed this workbook

Name of signatory ....

Position ....

Signature ....

Date ....

Official stamp

Fourth Edition

INSTITUTE OF LEADERSHIP & MANAGEMENT
SUPER SERIES
FOURTH EDITION

To order – phone us direct for prices and availability details
(please quote ISBNs when ordering) on 01865 888190